POODLE

SMART OWNER'S GUIDE™

FROM THE
EDITORS OF
DOGFANCY
MAGAZINE

CONTENTS

8-30-10

Poodle, a Smart Owner's Guide™
part of the Kennel Club Books® Interactive Series™
ISBN: 978-1-593787-73-8. ©2010

Kennel Club Books Inc., 40 Broad St., Freehold, NJ 07728. Printed in China.
All rights reserved. No part of this book may be reproduced in any form,
by Photostat, scanner, microfilm, xerography or any other means, or incorporated
into any information retrieval system, electronic or mechanical,
without the written permission of the copyright owner.

*photographers include Isabelle Francias/BowTie Inc.; Tara Darling/BowTie Inc.;
Gina Cioli and Pamela Hunnicutt/BowTie Inc. Contributing writer: Charlotte Schartz*
For CIP information, see page 176.

If you have taken a poodle into your home from a responsible breeder or a rescue group — or are planning to do so — congratulations! You have fallen in love with one of the most intelligent, versatile and charming breeds in all of dogdom.

Although today's poodle makes an elegant show dog in his flamboyant clip, under that fancy 'do beats the heart of a water retriever. In fact, the poodle was first clipped for utilitarian reasons: hair up front to keep his heart, lungs and joints warm; his back end shorn to give him more freedom for swimming. Given half a chance, poodles can still work as proficient water retrievers and even those of the Miniature variety have earned hunting titles.

However, the poodle has a clownish side as well. He can be a total ham and loves to perform for an appreciative audience, be it a circus act, an obedience routine, a victory lap around the show ring or a repertoire of parlor tricks. This breed has such a sense of humor and style that breeders have coined an adjective to capture the essence of the breed: poodley. A poodley dog carries himself proudly, well coiffed and prancing down the street with his head and tail held high. Although the poodle originated in Germany, not France, he exudes a definite *joie de vivre*, a zest for life.

The poodle also offers owners lots of options … in size, coat and color. The large, or Standard, poodle is the oldest of the three

varieties: a fine swimmer, alert watch dog and strong, high-spirited athlete. He makes a fine city dog but needs plenty of exercise. While the American Kennel Club specifies a height of more than 15 inches, most Standard Poodles today are in the 25-inch range. The Toy, at 10 inches or less, and the Miniature, taller than 10 inches to a maximum of 15 inches, make perfect apartment dogs. Historically, these sizes were used in England, Spain and Germany to dig up that great fungus delicacy known as the truffle.

For show purposes, poodles older than one year of age must be exhibited in either the English Saddle clip or the Continental clip. These are the intricate cuts that feature the tall topknot on the head, the pompons on the legs, the big coat at the front end and the shaved back end. Occasionally, ambitious exhibitors cord their poodles' coats, which is the painstaking process of pulling the hair apart by hand into dreadlocks. Corded poodles were far more common in the early days of showing the breed.

While dog-show exhibitors are limited in their choices, pet owners can select from dozens of clips, including short, all-over-curly cuts that aren't the least bit *froufrou*. The poodle coat feels like human hair and, like human hair, continues to grow. Clipping is recommended every eight weeks. It's not cheap but, on the upside, no shedding dog hair will be left on your clothes and furniture.

Poodles come in an array of attractive solid colors from black, white and various shades of brown to gray, silver, apricot, mahogany red and cream. Patched and multi-colored poodles also exist. Although these are not permitted in the AKC show

With this Smart Owner's Guide™, you are well on your way to getting your poodle diploma. But your poodle education doesn't end here.

You're invited to join in **Club Poodle™ (DogChannel.com/Club-Poodle)**, a FREE online site with lots of fun and instructive features such as:

◆ **forums, blogs** and **profiles** where you can connect with other poodle owners

◆ **downloadable charts** and **checklists** to help you be a smart and loving poodle owner

◆ access to poodle **e-cards** and **wallpapers**

◆ interactive **games**

◆ canine **quizzes**

The **Smart Owner's Guide** series and **Club Poodle** are backed by the experts at DOG FANCY® magazine and DogChannel.com — who have been providing trusted and up-to-date information about dogs and dog people for more than 40 years. Log on and join the club today!

ring, they may be exhibited at United Kennel Club dog shows. Affectionate, stylish and amazingly intelligent, poodles of all sizes are a pleasure to know and a joy to live with.

Allan Reznik,
Editor-at-Large, DOG FANCY

PLEASERS

Whatever his size — Standard, Miniature or Toy — poodles are athletic, agile dogs that need some outlet for their abundant energy and superior smarts. The poodle is also a people pooch who loves to socialize and hang out with his human family. But is this breed, in his three varieties, the right breed for you and your family? If so, which size is best for you? Let's find out, starting with the Toy and the Miniature.

THE TOY AND THE MINI

Life is never dull with a Toy or Miniature Poodle. Like their big brother, the Standard Poodle, they're active, athletic dogs that excel in most every canine sport, from agility to rally. They also make wonderful therapy dogs. When it comes to dog sports and activities, there isn't much of anything that a poodle can't do, given the right training. Exuberant and enthusiastic, poodles view the world as their stage, with humans as the adoring audience to their performance. None of this is surprising for a breed that once made his living as a circus performer.

Because they've lived and worked so closely with people as companions and performers, Toy and Miniature Poodles are highly sensitive to human needs and wants. That's one of the reasons they're such great pets, says Dorrit Diehl of Sheboygan, Wisc., a member of the Greater Milwaukee (Wisc.) Poodle Club.

Although the poodle in general — there's no such thing as an "average" poodle — is a proud, intelligent and dignified dog with a strong sense of self, each has his own spe-cial personality. Some are happy-go-lucky, smart but not inquisitive, and others display a high level of intelligence and curiosity that often lands them in trouble. "Most of the [behavior] problems I see with poodles stem from the fact that they are very, very intelligent," Diehl says.

HIGH ENERGY LEVEL

You might think that their size qualifies Toy and Miniature Poodles as perfect apartment or condo dogs. With the right owner, that might be true. However, Kari Winters of North Hills, Calif., shares her life with two Toy Poodles, Katie and Kelsie, and she believes that her dogs are too loud and energetic for that lifestyle. Katie and Kelsie have a big backyard, but even so, they really love to go for walks.

"Their energy level is extremely high," Winters says. "Katie loves to race around the bed at high speed, then reverse direction. She's also fond of removing the stuffing from her toys. We have an agreement. If it's her toy, she can destroy it if she

> **it's a Fact**
>
> **Poodles come in a variety of colors:** blues, grays, silvers, browns, *café-au-laits*, apricots, creams and more. The color, however, should be an even, solid color or a coat in varying shades of the same color. The poodle should not have a coat of two or more different colors.

wants to, but she can't chew anything that's not hers. Amazingly, she's good about it. Kelsie likes cat toys, such as mice and catnip things."

Toy Poodles like playing with all kinds of squeaky toys, rattles and even empty paper towel rolls, says Ianthe Bloomquist of Palmetto, Fla., who has bred and shown Toy Poodles. "Some will chase a toy or ball as long as your arm holds out."

Cathy Catelain from Cary, Ill., says her Minis are also active. They like to grab and shake stuffed toys, chase tennis balls and flying discs and chew on edible bones and rawhides. "They like to be kept active, and they play with each other," she says. "They'll play tug-of-war, or one will pick up a toy and run with it. In the yard, they run around and chase each other."

What poodles like best, however, is an elegant stroll that allows them to strut their stuff. It's easy to imagine them promenading along Paris' *Champs d'Elysees*. "You can do a brisk walk with them, but they would much prefer to stop and see all the dogs, kids and other people in the neighborhood," Catelain says. "They're extremely social dogs."

Clearly, Mini and Toy Poodles aren't simply decorative dogs that look good on the sofa. They need challenges to their intelligence and energy level. Positive reinforcement in the form of praise, along with con-

sistency in training and expectations, works best with poodles. These dogs are sensitive, so it's important not to make them feel bad. On the other hand, it's all too easy to let these smart dogs manipulate you into letting them do what they want, rather than what you want. Be firm, and try not to laugh at their attempts at distraction, at least not in their presence.

High energy level aside, poodles are happy to cuddle on the sofa as long as they can be with their people. "They're active

Poodles of all sizes love to be active. Dog sports, such as agility, make great outlets for their energy.

Meet other poodle owners just like you. On our poodle forums, you can chat about your poodle and ask other owners for advice on training, health issues and anything else about your favorite dog breed. Log onto **DogChannel.com/Club-Poodle** for details!

Poodles can be lap dogs at times; just make sure they get plenty of exercise during the day!

dogs, but when I want to sit on the couch and watch television, they just want to be up there next to me," Catelain says. "They all lie down in a row. They're quiet when you want them to be quiet, and active when you want them to be active."

Poodles can, however, develop behavior problems if their people give in to the desire to spoil them rather than provide them with the training and discipline they need to become good companions. They have a reputation for being yappy and have a habit of jumping on people. But both of those behaviors can be curbed with proper training.

Although all poodles can have their bad-behavior moments, housetraining is where they shine. Poodles are very easy to housetrain: They want to be clean, they don't want to be in a dirty crate or pen, and they're very good about telling you if they have to go out.

HIGH MAINTENANCE

There's a lot to consider before deciding to acquire a Toy or Mini Poodle, but the most important thing to know is that they are high-maintenance dogs. Just in case it's not clear from looking at a poodle's curly coat, this dog needs to be groomed on a regular basis. Even if you keep your Toy or Mini Poodle's coat trimmed short, it still needs to be brushed regularly.

Poodles love to look good. If they were people, they'd be supermodels showing off the latest fashion designs. But like some supermodels, they might pretend to disdain or even dislike the whole beautification process.

On the upside, when poodle hair falls out — and poodles do shed to some extent, no matter what you may have heard to the contrary — it usually sticks in the coat rather than falling onto the floor or floating onto furniture and clothing. That's because the woolly poodle has a crooked hair shaft. It's also one of the reasons it's so important to brush poodles regularly. If you don't remove the hairs that have fallen out, mats and tangles form.

The good news is that poodles don't shed a lot of hair all at once, the way most other breeds do. Their hair has a long growth cycle and falls out a little at a time throughout the year. If you keep it clipped regularly, you shouldn't have a problem with any dog hairs on your furniture, clothes, etc. They also don't appear to shed a great deal of dander. This may be why some people who are allergic to dogs can tolerate poodles quite well.

THE STANDARD

The Standard Poodle's retrieving roots have resulted in a highly active dog that needs an owner who can keep up. "They're extremely athletic dogs," says Sherry Bryant, former president of the Tidelands Poodle Club of Virginia.

A wise poodle owner will channel his or her dog's athleticism into acceptable out-

lets, such as canine sports. Bryant began competing her dog, Toula, in agility. Within a few short months, Toula had earned her American Kennel Club Novice Agility title and began working on adding more titles to that achievement.

Other owners have taken more unorthodox routes to helping their dogs discharge excess energy. For example, Alaska resident John Suter literally harnessed his Standard Poodles' talents. In the late 1980s, he raced his team of poodles — dubbed "Spirit Poodles" by a friend — in the grueling Iditarod sled dog race. This unusual team never won the race, but they finished each of the three times that Suter entered them. By finishing, they proved to have more endurance than many teams of northern breeds that traditionally dominate the sport, many of which quit before the end of the race.

However, a Standard Poodle need not compete in formal sports to get sufficient exercise. A daily romp at the dog park, some play with a canine friend, a brisk walk or a fetch session in a fenced yard each day can keep this dog mellow and

Poodle puppies are very intelligent and shouldn't be difficult to housetrain.

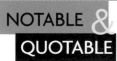

NOTABLE & QUOTABLE *A poodle's tail is one of the best indications of the pup's temperament and health. If it's not straight up, something is wrong.* — Ann Kennedy of Stockton, Calif., an American Kennel Club judge who has bred and finished more than 100 champions

Poodles love to be around other dogs, especially other poodles.

happy. Maryln Brooks, a breeder from Phoenix, Az., recommends that Standard Poodle owners "have a large yard where [the dog] can run and play, or be taken on long, daily — or at least biweekly — hikes."

STANDARDS LOVE PEOPLE

The Standard Poodle's eagerness to please reflects what devotees agree is the central fact of this breed's life: The poodle adores the people he lives with.

"Poodles are just so anxious to be with you at all times," says Standard Poodle breeder Marion Banta from Asbury, N.J. "Poodles are constantly underfoot. When I'm working in the kitchen, the dogs are all lying at my feet trying to get as close as possible. When I go into another room it's a parade of poodles!"

Brooks agrees. "Poodles actually think that they're people," she says. "They'll follow you from room to room as you clean house, and don't wish to be left outside."

Poodles are one of the smartest dogs. They take on different roles for different people in order to meet their needs. They know when you're happy or sad. They know when you're sick, and they take care of you. And there's nothing more beautiful than a poodle in show coat all done up. Whether they win or lose, they take your breath away. — Mini owner Cathy Catelain from Cary, Ill.

The operative word in Brooks's statement, of course, is "left." When the poodle's special person is also outside, the poodle is happy to be there. A case in point is the legendary Boye, a white Standard Poodle who was the companion of Prince Rupert of the Palinate (1619–1682), who was a gifted military commander of the English Civil War during the seventeenth century. Boye apparently exhibited the Standard Poodle's usual Velcro-dog characteristics: He accompanied his master not only to the battlefield but also to church, military councils and meals. He even stayed with Rupert for the three years the prince was in prison. But Boye didn't confine his love to his master. He also was devoted to Rupert's uncle, King Charles I of England (1600–1649), who returned the dog's affection wholeheartedly. In fact, Boye was a great favorite among the soldiers under Rupert's command, who attributed their many early victories to Boye's presence.

According to Banta, poodles can fall in love with just about anyone. "Poodles are extremely adaptable," she says. "They just love to be with people who love them. They can fit into a household full of young children or live with a couple of retirees."

Poodle breeder Linda Caldwell from Burrell, Pa., agrees. "All of my dogs have never met a stranger, and they love everyone," she says. "I take them to work with me quite frequently, and they visit my mother in the nursing home. They love the residents there and are very tolerant of everyone, including my grandchildren, who lay all over them and hug and kiss them constantly."

That tolerance extends to the show ring, too. "Every poodle I've met on the show circuit has been so friendly and sweet," Caldwell says. "There can be problems in any breed, but as a whole, I think the poodle temperament is wonderful. Hundreds of folks have passed my dogs on a grooming table at dog shows. If they get close enough, they get a big wet kiss; if they aren't that close, they merely get a paw on the arm or shoulder."

Twenty-first century Standard Poodle owners have found that their dogs are even willing to put their people ahead of themselves. Bryant believes that poodles would do better in the agility ring if they had less of a partnership ethic. "If the handler has a problem on the agility course, the poodle tries to compensate for the handler's performance, unlike a lot of Border Collies that continue working the course with or without the handler," Bryant explains. "This is why so many poodles slow down in agility."

Poodles are smart, sympathetic, sweet and sure to be your best pal — no matter their size!

Bentley Gets a New Ride

Marie Bennington of Athens, Ga., wanted a "Velcro" dog (a dog that would stick with her), and she knew she wanted that dog to be a poodle. When she found Bentley, she knew he'd be a great match for her family. The 70-pound Standard Poodle-mix had been found wandering the streets of Atlanta, starving, badly matted and in desperate need of veterinary care.

Bennington called Atlanta Pet Rescue, where Bentley was fostered, and discovered that he was a wonderful dog, but that he was mouthy and tended to bite hands. Bennington, a dog owner all her life, wasn't concerned. She knew that Bentley just wanted attention.

She filled out the adoption application and the rescue called to ask questions. Bennington is a truck driver, and the rescue volunteers were concerned that the dog wouldn't like being cooped up in a semi truck's cab for long periods, and they feared that he wouldn't get enough exercise. Fortunately for both truck driver and dog, federal law requires that drivers have 10 hours off daily, which leaves plenty of time for long walks. When at home, Bentley would have free run of the property to chase squirrels.

"They called our family vet to check that our two dogs had their shots and asked questions about how we cared for our pets," Bennington says. "We provided other references, as well, so they could talk to people who know us and could tell them how we treat our pets. This important work is mostly done by volunteers, to ensure that a dog is placed in a home that will properly care for him and not neglect him. Many dogs in rescues have socialization or behavioral problems, so rescue groups screen the applicants carefully to ensure that the person who adopts a particular dog is knowledgeable and capable of handling that dog's particular issues. After all the screening was done, we were approved!"

Bentley still gets mouthy, but he's getting much better with the positive training that the Benningtons give him in his new home. "He spends a lot of time with our children and feels the need to keep them in sight as much as possible," Bennington says.

Bentley went from a sad situation to a loving family, bringing plenty of joy to his new family. "He still has the poodle sense of humor that endears this breed to everyone who meets one," she says.

THE TOPIC OF TOYS

This Toy has the biggest cuteness factor, and he certainly likes to be played with!

COUNTRY OF ORIGIN: Germany

WHAT HIS FRIENDS CALL HIM: Tiny, Small Fry, Poo-poo

GROUP: Toy

SIZE: up to 10 inches tall; 5 to 7 pounds

COAT & COLOR: The harsh and curly coat can be kept natural, corded or clipped and comes in a uniform color, including apricot, black, blue, cream, gray, silver or white.

PERSONALITY TRAITS: intelligent, highly trainable, more sensitive than Standards

WITH KIDS: may be too tiny for very young children

WITH OTHER PETS: fine, if properly socialized

LIFESPAN: 12 to 14 years

A MINIATURE MOMENT

Portable and petite, this mini poodle is the most popular.

COUNTRY OF ORIGIN: Germany

WHAT HIS FRIENDS CALL HIM:
Bozo, Happy, Wallenda, Mini Me

GROUP: Non-Sporting

SIZE: 11 to 15 inches tall;
14 to 16 pounds

COAT & COLOR: The harsh and curly coat can be kept natural, corded or clipped and comes in a uniform color, including apricot, black, blue, cream, gray, silver or white.

PERSONALITY TRAITS: intelligent, highly trainable, more sensitive than Standards

WITH KIDS: no problems here

WITH OTHER PETS: fine, if properly socialized

LIFESPAN: 10 to 13 years

STANDARD IN SHORT

There's nothing standard about this Standard.

COUNTRY OF ORIGIN: Germany

WHAT HIS FRIENDS CALL HIM:
Big Boy, Andre, Pierre, Curly

GROUP: Non-Sporting

SIZE: More than 15 inches tall; 45 to 70 pounds

COAT & COLOR: double coated, with a curly, harsh outer coat. It may be clipped or corded. Colors include apricot, black, blue, cream, gray, silver, brown, *café au lait* or white.

PERSONALITY TRAITS: intelligent, highly trainable. He is affectionate with friends and family but can be aloof toward strangers.

WITH KIDS: very well

GROOMING: To keep the coat mat-free, it should be brushed daily and clipped regularly, at least four times a year. Special care should be taken to keep the poodle's long, thickly feathered ears clean and free from infection.

ENERGY LEVEL: high

SPECIAL NEEDS: exercise, professional grooming, training

LIFESPAN: 10 to 13 years

CHAPTER 2

THE POODLE'S

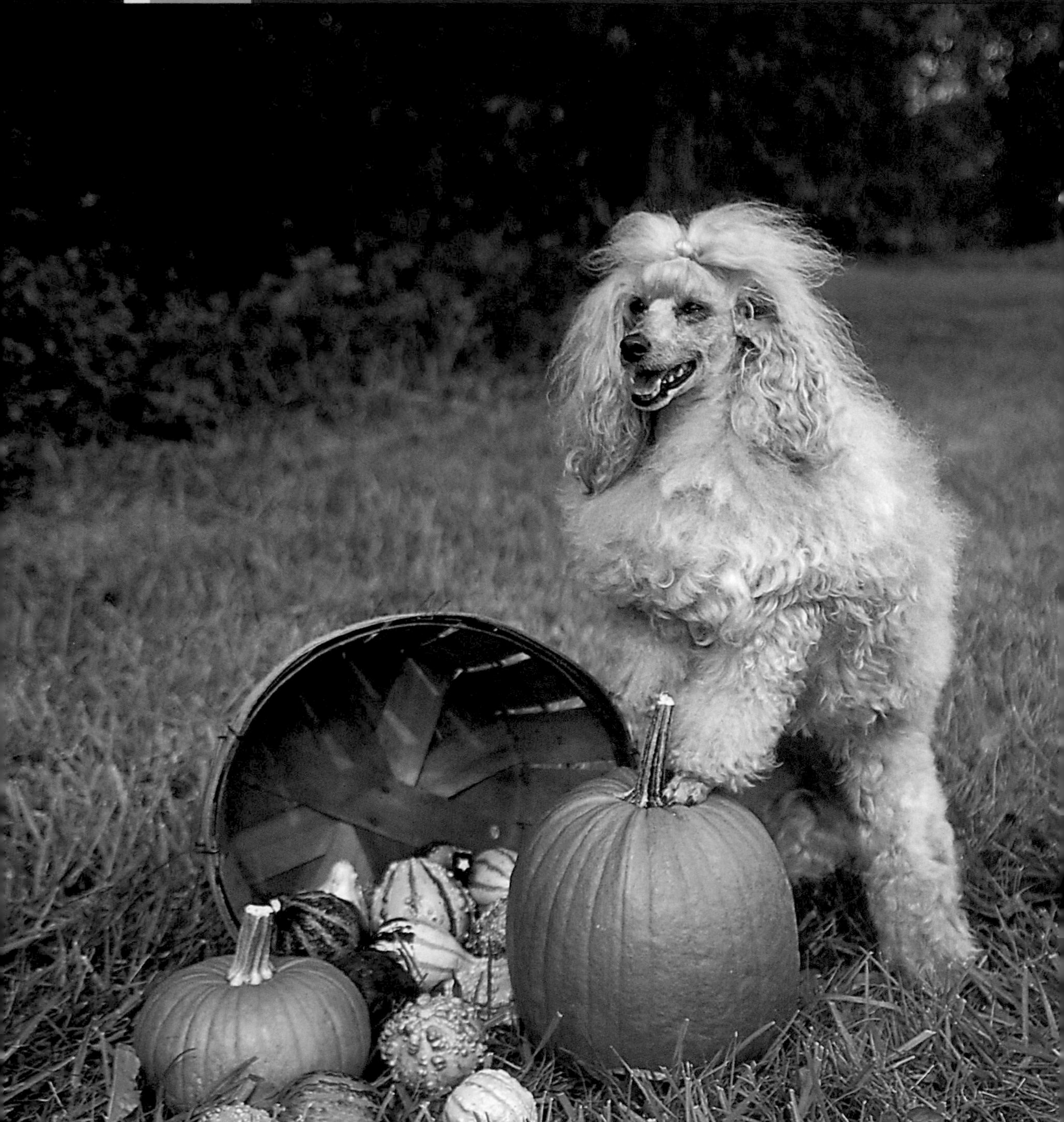

PAST

A strong, supple, canine swimmer paddles through the sparkling water of an ancient lake, retrieving a duck in his mouth. His muscled hindquarters ripple, his face projects an alert intelligence and as he scrambles to shore and shakes off the water, his thick coat of water-repellent curls seems to dry in an instant.

Where could this lake have been and when did this poodle live? The first curly-coated dog with a penchant for duck hunting might have come from Germany, or France, or Russia, or maybe even ancient Rome. Many people theorize about the poodle's origins, but we do know one thing for sure: People have admired, worked with and bred poodle-like dogs for centuries all across Europe. Let's look at some of the historical clues to how the poodle, in all three sizes — Standards, Toy and Miniature — and a rainbow of colors — blues, grays, silvers, browns, blacks, to name a few — became the intelligent, athletic and almost-human companion we know and love today.

Did You Know? **Fluffed and coiffed, poodles have a look that says "Pamper me, *oui*?"** The truth about the national dog of France is that beneath all that hair, there's a ruggedly-built water retriever that's extremely qualified to help others. In fact, poodles excel at dog-assisted therapy, bringing comfort and joy to the sick, injured and elderly.

WHICH CAME FIRST

The first historical sign of a curly-coated dog with clipped hindquarters — a likely ancestor to the poodle, as well as the Portuguese Water Dog and the Irish Water Spaniel — appears on a Roman tomb dated about A.D. 40. It wasn't until more than 1,000 years later, however, that evidence of poodle-like dogs began to show up in art and literature.

By the 15th century, curly-coated dogs with clipped coats had already integrated into the cultures of many European countries and appeared in paintings and illuminated manuscripts from France, Holland and Italy. Albrecht Durer (1471 to 1528) depicted German poodles in some of his drawings, and in 18th century Spain, the artist Goya (1746 to 1828) included poodles in some of his paintings during a time when poodles were popular in Spain. Also, when Louis XVI held the throne in France (from 1774 to 1792), Toy Poodles were among the aristocracy's most-favored pets.

Although many historians believe the Standard Poodle came first, the Toy Poodle was likely evolving at about the same time. By the time we see poodles represented in art, the three sizes already existed. As was typical with dogs before the advent of dog shows, size and type weren't standardized, so large and small dogs could sometimes come from a single litter. Larger dogs were probably used more for working, and smaller dogs were typically handed over to the ladies for companionship.

In France, the smaller poodle-type dogs were called "*petit barbet*" and resembled their larger Barbet cousins much less than today's Toy Poodles resemble Standard Poodles. Many of these small white dogs were probably related to other small white dogs at the time, including the Bichon Frise and Maltese. If all these small white dogs evolved together, the Toy Poodle comes from ancient lines. In England during the 18th century, a small white Toy Poodle-type dog called the "White Cuban" came into fashion, which may be an ancestor of the Toy Poodle today.

The largest poodles were sometimes called "*grand barbet*," "*caniche*," "*mouton*," "*moufflon*" or "*canis aviarius aquaricus*" in France, and the familiar "*pudel*" in German. The German *pudel* was heavier in build, more muscular and athletic, but the Russian poodle more closely resembled the Greyhound in his shape and slender build. In England, an early water dog also resembled the poodle.

Most people consider Germany the breed's country of origin; certainly, this is where the poodle got his name. In German, *pudel* means "to splash around in the water." Still, France may have popularized the poodle more than any other country, making the poodle its national dog and going to great

it's a Fact

The three varieties of poodles — Toy, Miniature and Standard — vary in size, but the bone and muscle of both forelegs and hind legs should be in proportion to the dog's size. A poodle of any variety should have a squarely built appearance, meaning the length of his body, when measured from the breastbone to the rump, should be about the same size as the height from his withers (shoulders) to the ground.

The poodle is the aristocrat of the dog world!

lengths throughout the centuries to refine and beautify the poodle's distinctive haircuts.

Throughout these early years in Europe, poodles were also typically styled in one of two ways: curly or corded into long ropes. Some sources divide these two poodles into two separate types, as if the coat itself differed in texture. Others believe that any poodle can be corded if the coat is handled correctly, and that corded and noncorded coats aren't any different beyond the method of styling. In the 19th century, corded coats were so popular that most poodles had them, especially in England.

UNMISTAKABLE

Of all the purebred dogs in the world, the poodle is among the most easily recognizable. Poodles certainly resemble other less well-known water dogs, but nobody mistakes a poodle for an Irish Water Spaniel; it's much more likely to be the other way around. The poodle has his unique look and style for particular reasons directly related to his history and original purpose.

The water retriever's unique haircut was designed to keep his internal organs warm in the cold water, but the hair was shaved off of his back end so that the thick coat wouldn't become too heavy and impede the dog in the water. Today's cuts, based on that same principle, are admittedly fancier and not so utilitarian; quite frankly, it's now a matter of fashion.

Beyond the coat, the poodle is also built for the jobs he performed. The poodle's strong, muscular hindquarters, the back end angled for swimming and the deep chest suited for endurance work help the poodle excel in the water. His keen eyes and long jaws also contributed to his retrieving skills. These qualities, along with the curly coat common to all the water dogs, may be evidence that all these breeds are related.

The poodle's self-confident, outgoing nature and eagerness to work also suited him for many other functions. "A poodle that lacks a love of water, a keen natural retrieve and a do-anything, go-anywhere spirit entirely lacks correct temperament," says Emily Cain of Jerseyville, Canada, a poodle owner and member of the Poodle Club of Canada. "Of course, the dog also has to possess the conformation to enable the various jobs," she adds.

Those jobs, historically, have been numerous. Early Standard Poodles pulled carts, retrieved birds and generally helped on the hunt. Poodles of all sizes distinguished themselves as circus performers; their intelligence, easy trainability and agile, athletic figures made them naturals at flips, somersaults and playacting, complete with costumes.

Mr. Crawley, a famous British showman, had a "Ball of Little Dogs" that performed for Queen Anne (1665-1714), and many poodles were active in French circuses. In fact, throughout the 19th century, little troupes of performing dogs entertained people in England, France, Italy and Germany.

Smaller poodles — rumored to be crossed with a terrier, but this isn't documented —

Our poodle Chloe is 10 pounds of complete devotion. She curls into a tight ball next to you for a nap and will not disturb you. She observes all household activities from a comfortable spot on the couch, and if you join her there, she will roll onto her back as an invitation to rub her belly! — Nancy Larkin of Mission Veijo, Calif.

Westminster Best In Show winners include: Standard Poodle Int. Ch. Nunsoe Duc de la Terracre in 1938; Miniature Poodle Ch. Pitter Patter of Piperscroft in 1943; Toy Poodle Ch. Wilber White Swan in 1956; Standard Poodle Ch. Puttencove Promise in 1958; Miniature Poodle Ch. Fontclair Festoon in 1959; Toy Poodle Ch. Cappoquin Little Sister in 1961; Standard Poodle Ch. Acadia Command Performance in 1973; Standard Poodle Ch. Whisperwind On A Carousel in 1991; and Miniature Poodle Ch. Surrey Spice Girl in 2002.

were trained to hunt for truffles, that valuable fungus that grows underground and is prized in gourmet cooking. The dogs were taught to sniff them out and dig them up, and they had particularly keen scenting ability and a penchant for digging. Because truffle hunting was usually done at night, these small poodles were typically white, enabling their handlers to spot them easily.

During the Napoleonic Wars (1799 to 1815), many poodles died defending their masters in battle. One poodle named Magrita carried a sack of bandages around his neck to aid wounded soldiers. Another well-known black poodle named Moustache was awarded the full rank and pay of a French soldier after unwinding the French flag from a dying soldier and carrying it — proudly waving — back to the front lines of the battle. For this, Moustache was also awarded a medal of gallantry and was permitted to

Poodles of the Past

Everybody notices a poodle when he prances down the street, but some poodles have truly distinguished themselves above all others. Check out these most influential poodles and imagine what it might be like to brush curls with greatness.

■ Henri III (1551 to 1589), king of France, had three favorite poodle-type dogs named Liline, Titi and Mimi, whom he carried in a basket around his neck. When the Dominican friar Jacques Clement tried to assassinate the king, the three poodles barked to warn him.

■ Poet Alexander Pope (1688 to 1744) owned Marquis, a *"caniche"* (French poodle). Marquis once saved his master's life when Pope's valet tried to murder him. The story goes that Pope awoke to noise and found three robbers in his garden, with his poodle holding the valet down by the throat. The valet held a gun and had intended to rob and murder Pope.

■ Rufus was Winston Churchill's (1874 to 1965) Miniature Poodle. Several famous photographs depict them together, including one in which Rufus is leaping chin-high to greet his beloved master.

■ Jazz singer Billie Holiday (1915 to 1959) had a Standard Poodle that, upon the dog's death, she wrapped in her best mink coat for his cremation.

■ Ch. Chieveley Chopstick, a black Miniature Poodle, was the first Mini to earn the title of Champion during the same year that the American Kennel Club recognized Miniatures as a poodle variety in 1932.

■ Ch. Whippendell Poli of Carillon was a black Standard Poodle and the first poodle to win the AKC Non-Sporting Group at the Westminster Kennel Club Dog Show in 1933.

■ Several notable poodles appear in the 2000 film *Best in Show*: Can. Ch. Exxel Dezi Duz It With Pizzaz, owned and bred by Suzanne Warrington of Bellingham, Wash., appears in some of the early scenes. Brocade Exclamation is used in the Group and BIS scenes. Porsche was bred by Gloria and Steve Walkley and Jeff Burmeister of Olympia, Wash., and owned by Kevin Patton, Burmeister and Gloria Walkley. Can. Ch. Valcopy Sheer Glamour is the Toy Poodle in the movie who wins 2nd in the Group. She was bred by Dana Plonkey and owned by Plonkey and Beth Hilborn of Vancouver, Canada.

wear a dog collar bearing the tricolors of the French flag and his engraved silver medal. When he was eventually killed by a cannon blast, the dog was buried and a tombstone erected with an epitaph that read "Brave."

In 1942, a poodle breeder named Arlene Erlanger from Elberon, N.J., came up with the notion that dogs should help in the World War II effort and helped to found Dogs for Defense, which recruited and

trained suitable dogs for guarding munitions plants and forts, and working with soldiers overseas. Standard Poodles were among the list of acceptable breeds until 1944, when the list was cut to five breeds and the German Shepherd Dog became the U.S. Army's official breed.

AMERICAN POODLES

As early as the 19th century, people in North America knew about poodles — Standards as well as Toys — but they were relatively rare and considered two separate breeds. In 1931, the Poodle Club of America was formed to help standardize and organize the breed; they wrote a breed standard describing in detail the way the poodle should look. At this time, the PCA considered the Standard Poodle and Toy Poodle to be separate breeds.

The first Toy Poodles in America looked substantially different from those of today. They were more akin to the other small, white European breeds, such as the Bichon Frise and Maltese. Some people speculate that all these toy breeds were interbred and are related.

When the Miniature Poodle came onto the scene in America, fanciers wanted to show them in dog shows, too. In 1932, the PCA recognized the Miniature Poodle as a variety of poodle, and these little fellows had to compete against the Standards. The poodles were grouped into two coat types: curly and corded. In 1943, the PCA accepted Toy Poodles as a third variety, and breeders worked to standardize the look of the Toy Poodle. Today, the Toy much more closely resembles the Standard Poodle, and the breed standards for all three are identical, except for size.

When a white Standard Poodle named Triple Int. Ch. Nunsoe Duc de la Terrace of

You have an unbreakable bond with your dog, but do you always understand him? Go online and download "Dog Speak," which outlines how dogs communicate. Find out what your poodle is saying when he barks, howls or growls. Go to **DogChannel.com/Club-Poodle** and click on "Downloads."

Blakeen came to America in 1933, the dog show really world took notice; this dog not only won the AKC Non-Sporting Group at the Westminster Kennel Club Dog Show in 1934 but also won Best In Show at Westminster in 1935, the first poodle to take this prestigious honor. His handler, Hayes Blake Hoyt, was the first woman ever to stand in that famous ring at Madison Square Garden in New York City, holding the lead of a BIS candidate.

Suddenly, poodles were the royalty of the dog show world, and their popularity exploded. Since that first poodle victory at Westminster, eight other poodles have won BIS at the America's oldest dog show.

Poodles have come a long way since their hard-working water-retrieving days, but today's poodle still shines in the show ring, boasts a unique curly coat and has the intelligence and exuberance to do almost any job, from retrieving and tracking to agility and therapy work. "A poodle with a correct temperament should have all the characteristics pertaining to all the traditional roles," Cain says. "First, the poodle has to be able to do those jobs. Then, it has to have the temperament to perform the jobs. And finally, it has to have the conformation that makes the jobs easy to perform."

OH, THAT HAIR!

The poodle's distinctive haircut may have working roots, but since those early days of water retrieving in Europe, fashions have changed, and so has the poodle's 'do. Once the poodle caught on in fashion-conscious France, fanciful poodle trimming became all the rage, peaking at the turn of the 20th century, particularly in Paris and London. Poodles are one of the few breeds that can truly become a canine friend who can boast your fashionability, due to their amazingly changeable, shapeable coats! They can even be trimmed to match the cut and style of your outfit, as many poodles belonging to aristocratic women once were.

Some people believe the poodle's fancy pompon on the end of his tail was designed by the French to mock the English lion, and fancy has been a big part of the history of the poodle's haircuts. In turn-of-the-century Paris and London, poodle groomers set up shop on street corners. Customers' poodles became canvases; the groomers their artists.

"Poodles were trimmed with hand trimmers in all kinds of fantastic patterns," says Shirlee Kalstone, author of *Poodle Clipping and Grooming: An International Reference* (Howell Book House, 2000). Groomers trimmed the poodles' tails to look like flags, and shaped their heads to give them moustaches and long, pointed beards. People could request any design, and many asked for shamrocks, thistles, family crests, sporting themes and current events to be clipped into the poodle's constantly growing coat. These could be touched up or changed every month or so, as the coat grew out.

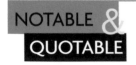

Poodles are smart and, in my opinion, almost human. They know what you are thinking and what you are going to do before you do it. They are wonderful, loving companions.

— *Miniature and Toy Poodle owner Mary Ann Smith of Laguna Niguel, Calif.*

One enterprising groomer regularly attended horse races, then quickly trimmed the crest of the winning horse on the back of a poodle. "He would then rush to the track and sell the poodle to the horse's owner, who was of course hugely impressed and was happy to buy the dog," Kalstone says.

Many show dogs at the turn of the century wore corded coats, a fashion at the time. These cords form naturally in the poodle's curly coat, but groomers often shaped and defined the cords by coating them with paraffin. "There was really a madness for corded poodles at this time," Kalstone says. "People used to tie up their poodles' cords with leather straps so the cords wouldn't touch the ground, and many people have written that the corded poodles smelled horrible because they were never washed."

In the show ring, cuts have evolved from long cords to shaggy haircuts with shaved rear-ends to the many cuts acceptable today, complete with pompons and glamour, each including a topknot: Here are some of the common poodle cuts available today:

■ **Puppy Show Clip:** a long coat; the face, throat, feet and base of tail are shaved; pompon at the end of the tail

■ **English Saddle Clip:** The face, throat, feet, forelegs and base of the tail are shaved, with puffs on the forelegs and a pompon at the end of the tail; hindquarters are covered with a short blanket of hair.

■ **Continental Clip:** This is the show-ring standard, with the face, throat, paws and part of the tail shaved.

■ **Sporting Clip:** The face, feet, throat and base of tail are shaved; scissored cap on top of the head; pompon at the end of the tail.

■ **Other clips**: Pet owners sometimes choose other clips such as the Kennel Clip, Dutch Clip, Bikini Clip and Puppy Pet Clip. Some people even like to dye their poodle's hair shocking pink or other colors using temporary, pet-safe hair dye, but a quick look back at the turn of the century reveals that this practice is nothing new. Neither is poodle bling, as royalty used to bedeck their poodles in gem-encrusted collars and other jewelry that would probably out sparkle any pet jewelry you can buy today.

Part of the poodle's charm is his coat's ability to be shaped and styled into fanciful or fun haircuts. So whether your poodle is hot pink, corded or smartly cut short and neat, consider the history of that unique coat and the way poodles have echoed — and even been on the forefront — of human fashion.

A PUPPY

As rough and tumble as the poodle can be, nothing is cuter than a Standard, Miniature or Toy Poodle puppy. His sweet face and round little body inspire *oohs* and *ahhs* from all who see them. That wonderful endearing quality, however, can also distract you from taking the time and doing the legwork necessary to find a puppy who's not only adorable but also healthy in body and temperament. The key to finding the best poodle puppy for you is to resist being charmed into a hasty decision and wait to find a responsible breeder. Then, you can have fun picking just the right puppy from a litter of those lovable faces.

You're going to have your poodle — no matter the size — for at least a decade (or hopefully, longer!), so the time you spend early on to locate a healthy, well-adjusted puppy from a reputable breeder will definitely pay off in the long run. Look for a dedicated and ethical breeder who values good health and stable personalities, and who really cares what happens to the dog for the rest of his life.

it's a
Fact

Local breeder referrals are essential. A breeder who belongs to a local poodle club shows active involvement in the breed and breeds according to that particular club's code of ethics. That's who you want to do business with: a breeder who abides by a code of ethics.

Why is this so important? This breed has a unique personality and needs to be bred correctly by someone with experience who really knows what he or she is doing. If not, you may wind up with a dog who's overly aggressive, has a ton of health problems and doesn't even look like a poodle.

Be sure to avoid puppy mills and backyard breeders. Puppy mills are large-scale breeding operations that produce puppies in an assembly-line fashion without regard to health and socialization. Backyard breeders are typically well-meaning, regular pet owners who simply do not possess enough knowledge about the breed and breeding to produce healthy puppies.

The American Kennel Club and the United Kennel Club provide a list of breeders in good standing with their organizations. Visit their websites, listed in the Resources chapter on page 166, for more information.

EVALUATING BREEDERS

Once you have the names and numbers of breeders in your area, start contacting them to find out more about their breeding programs. But, before you contact them, prepare some questions to ask that will get you the information you need to know.

Prospective buyers interview breeders much the same way that a breeder should interview a buyer. Make a list of questions and record the answers so that you can compare them to the answers from other breeders whom you may interview later. The right questions are those that help you identify who has been in the breed a respectable number of years and who is actively showing their dogs. Ask in-depth questions regarding the genetic health of the pup's parents, grandparents and great grandparents. Ask what sort of genetic testing program the breeder adheres to.

You also should look to see if a breeder actively shows his or her dogs in conformation events (aka dog shows). Showing indicates that the breeder is bringing out examples from his or her breeding program for the public to see. If there are any obvious problems, such as temperament or general conformation, they will be readily apparent. Also, the main reason to breed poodles is to improve the quality of the breed. If the breeder is not showing, then he or she is more likely to be breeding purely for the monetary aspect and may have less concern for the welfare and future of the breed.

Inquiring about health and determining the breeder's willingness to work with you in the future are also important for the potential puppy buyer to learn. The prospective buyer should see what kind of health guarantees the breeder gives. You should also find out if the breeder will be available for future consultation regarding your poodle, and find out if the breeder will take your dog back if something unforeseen happens.

Prospective buyers should ask plenty of questions, and in return, buyers should also be prepared to answer questions posed by a responsible breeder who wants to make sure his or her puppy is going to a good home. Be

Did You Know?

Good Breeder Signs
When you visit a poodle breeder's home, look around the dwelling for:
• a clean, well-maintained facility
• no overwhelming odors
• an overall impression of cleanliness
• socialized dogs and puppies

NOTABLE & QUOTABLE *The most important use of a [puppy buyer's] contract is to make sure there is a clear understanding of everyone's rights and responsibilities. Hopefully, the contract can get dusty in the drawer, and your puppy can grow into a fun, healthy member of the family.* — Michael Wahlig of Long Lake, Mich., the foundation director for the Poodle Club of America

prepared for a battery of questions from the breeder regarding your purpose for wanting this breed of dog and whether you can properly care for one. Avoid buying from a breeder who does little or no screening. If a breeder doesn't ask any questions, they are not concerned with where their pups end up. In this case, the dogs' best interests are probably not the breeder's motive for breeding.

The buyer should find a breeder who is willing to answer any questions they have and are knowledgeable about the history of the breed, health issues and about the background of their own dogs. Learn about a breeder's long-term commitment to the poodle breed and to his or her puppies after they leave the kennel.

Look for breeders who know their purpose for producing a particular litter, those who are knowledgeable in the pedigrees of their dogs and of the poodle breed itself, and have had the necessary health screenings performed on the parents. They should also ask you for references to show that they are interested in establishing a relationship with you in consideration for a puppy. If after one phone conversation with a breeder, the person is supplying you with an address in which to send a deposit, continue your search for a reputable breeder elsewhere.

CHOOSING THE RIGHT PUP

Once you have found a breeder you are comfortable with, your next step is to pick the right puppy. The good news is that if you have done your homework and found a responsible breeder, you can count on this person to give you plenty of help in choosing the right pup for your personality and lifestyle. In fact, most good breeders will recommend a specific puppy once they know what kind of dog you want.

After you have narrowed down the search and selected a reputable breeder, rely on the experience of the breeder to help you select your puppy. The selection of the puppy depends a lot on what purpose the pup is being purchased for. If the pup is being purchased as a show prospect, the breeder will offer his or her assessment of the pups that meet this criteria and be able to explain the strengths and faults of each pup.

Whether your poodle puppy is show- or pet-quality, a good, stable temperament is vital for a happy relationship. Generally, you want to avoid a timid puppy or a very dominant one. Temperament is very important, and a reputable breeder should spend a lot of time with the pups and be able to offer an evaluation of each pup's personality.

A reputable breeder might tell you which poodle puppy is appropriate for your home situation and personality. They may not allow you to choose the puppy, but they will certainly take your preference into consideration.

Some breeders, on the other hand, believe it's important for you to be heavily involved in selecting a puppy from the litter. They will let their puppy buyers make

Did You Know?

Healthy puppies have clear eyes and shiny coats, and are playful and friendly. An important factor in a puppy's long-term health and good temperament is the age he goes to his permanent home, which should be between 8 and 10 weeks. This gives the puppies plenty of time to develop immunity and bond with their mom.

Questions to Expect
Be prepared for the breeder to ask you some questions, too.

JOIN OUR ONLINE
Club Poodle™

1. Have you previously owned a poodle?

The breeder is trying to gauge how familiar you are with the breed. If you have never owned one, illustrate your knowledge of poodles by telling the breeder about your research.

2. Do you have children? What are their ages?

Some breeders are wary about selling a dog to families with younger children.

This isn't a steadfast rule, and some breeders only insist on meeting the children to see how they handle puppies. It all depends on the breeder.

3. How long have you wanted a poodle?

This helps a breeder know if this purchase is an impulse buy or a carefully thought-out decision. Buying on impulse is one of the biggest mistakes owners can make. Be patient.

Join Club Poodle to get a complete list of questions a breeder should ask you. Click on "Downloads" at: **DogChannel.com/Club-Poodle**

the decision on which pup to take home because not everyone is looking for the same things in a dog. Some people want a quiet, laidback attitude. Others want an outgoing, active dog. When pups are old enough to go to their new homes at roughly 8 to 10 weeks of age, these breeders prefer you make your own decision because no one can tell at this age which pup will make the most intelligent or affectionate dog. The color, sex and markings are obvious, but that is about all you can tell for sure at this age. Everything else being equal — size, health, etc. — some breeders suggest picking the pup whom you have a gut feeling for.

The chemistry between a buyer and puppy is important and should play a role in determining which pup goes to which home. When possible, make numerous visits to see the puppies, and in effect, let a puppy choose you. There usually will be one puppy who spends more time with a buyer and is more comfortable relaxing and sitting with or on a person.

CHECKING FOR POODLE QUALITIES

Whether you are dealing with a breeder who wants to pick a pup for you or lets you make the decision alone, consider certain points when evaluating the pup who you may end up calling your own. The puppy should be friendly and outgoing, not skittish in any way. He should be forgiving of correction. He shouldn't be terribly mouthy. The pup should readily follow you and be willing to snuggle in your lap and be turned onto his back easily without a problem.

Proper temperament is very important. A poodle puppy who has a dominant personality requires an experienced owner who will be firm during training. A puppy

With the popularity of poodles — especially Toy and Miniatures — shelters and rescue groups across the country are often inundated with sweet, loving examples of the breed — from the tiniest puppies to

senior dogs, petite females to strapping males. Often, to get the poodle of your dreams, all it takes is a trip to the local shelter. Or, perhaps you could find your ideal dog waiting patiently in the arms of a foster parent at a nearby rescue group. It just takes a bit of effort, patience and a willingness to find the right dog for your family, not just the cutest dog on the block.

The perks of owning a poodle are plentiful: companionship, unconditional love, true loyalty and laughter, just to name a few. So why choose the adoption option? Because you will literally be saving a life!

Owners of adopted dogs swear they're more grateful and loving than any dog they've owned before. It's almost as if they knew what dire fate awaited them, and are so thankful to you. Poodles, known for their people-pleasing personalities, seem to embody this mentality wholeheartedly when they're rescued. And they want to give something back. Another perk: Almost all adopted dogs come fully vetted, with proper medical treatment and vaccinations, as well as being spayed or neutered. Some are even licensed and microchipped.

Don't disregard older dogs, thinking the only good pair-up is between you and a puppy. Adult poodles are more established behaviorally and personality-wise, helping to better mesh their characteristics with yours in this game of matchmaker. Puppies are always in high demand, so if you open your options to include adults, you will have a better chance of adopting quickly. Plus, adult dogs are often housetrained, more calm and chew-proof. And they don't need to be taken outside in the middle of the night ... five times ... in the pouring rain.

The Poodle Club of America offers rescue support information or log onto Petfinder.com. This site's searchable database enables you to find a poodle in your area who needs a break in the form of a compassionate owner like you. More websites are listed in the Resources chapter on page 166.

who is a little shy requires heavy socialization to build his confidence.

You also can evaluate a poodle puppy's temperament on your own. The temperament of the puppies can be evaluated by spending some time watching them. If you can visit the pups and observe them with their littermates, then you can see how they interact with each other. You may be able to pinpoint which ones are the bullies and which ones are more submissive.

In general, look for a puppy who is more interested in you than in his littermates. Then, take each poodle puppy individually to a new location away from the rest of the litter. Put the puppy down on the ground, walk away and see how he reacts to being away from the security of his mom and littermates. The puppy may be afraid at first, but he should gradually recover and start checking out the new surroundings.

D-I-Y TEMPERAMENT TEST

Standard, Miniature and Toy Poodle puppies come in a wide assortment of temperaments to suit almost everyone. If you are looking for a dog who is easily train-

able and a good companion to you and your family, you most likely want a puppy with a medium temperament.

Temperament testing can help you determine the type of disposition your potential poodle puppy possesses. A puppy who has a medium temperament will have the following reactions to these various tests, which are best conducted when the pup is 7 weeks old.

Step 1. To test a puppies' social attraction and his confidence in approaching humans, coax him toward you by kneeling down and clapping your hands gently. A pup with a medium temperament comes readily, tail up or down.

Step 2. To test a pup's eagerness to follow, walk away from him while he is watching you. He should follow you readily, tail up.

Step 3. To see how a pup handles restraint, kneel down and roll the pup gently on his back. Using a light but firm touch, hold him in this position with one hand for 30 seconds. The poodle pup should settle down after some initial struggle at first and offer some or steady eye contact.

Step 4. To evaluate a puppy's level of social dominance, stand up, then crouch down beside the pup and stroke him from head to back. A poodle puppy with a medium temperament — neither too dominant nor too submissive — should cuddle up to you and lick your face, or squirm and lick your hands.

Step 5. An additional test of a pup's dominance level is to bend over, cradle the pup under his belly with your fingers interlaced and palms up, and elevate him just off the ground. Hold him there for 30 seconds. The pup should not struggle and should be relaxed, or he should struggle and then settle down and lick you.

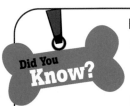

Breeder Q&A

Here are some questions you should ask a breeder and the answers you want.

Q. How often do you have litters available?

A. You want to hear "once or twice a year" or "occasionally" because a breeder who doesn't have litters that often is probably more concerned with the quality of the puppies, rather than with making money.

Q. What kinds of health problems do poodles have?

A. Beware of a breeder who says, "none." Every breed has health issues. For poodles, some health problems include idiopathic epilepsy, Addison's disease, sebaceous adenitis and progressive retinal atrophy.

Get a complete list of questions to ask a poodle breeder — and the ideal answers — at Club Poodle. Log onto **DogChannel.com/Club-Poodle** and click on "Downloads."

Food intolerance is the inability of a dog to completely digest certain foods. Puppies who may have done very well on their mother's milk may not do well on cow's milk. The result of this food intolerance may be loose bowels, passing gas and stomach pains. These are the only obvious symptoms of food intolerance, which makes diagnosis difficult.

PHYSICAL FEATURES

To assess a puppy's health, take a deliberate, thorough look at each part of his body. Signs of a healthy puppy include bright eyes, a healthy coat, a good appetite and firm stool.

Watch for a telltale link between physical and mental health. A healthy poodle, as with any breed of puppy, will display a happier, more positive attitude than an unhealthy puppy. A poodle puppy's belly should not be over extended or hard, as this may be a sign of worms. Also, if you are around the litter long enough to witness a bowel movement, the stool should be solid, and the pup should

When selecting a poodle puppy from a litter, try to find the one that seems to have a connection with you.

not show any signs of discomfort. Look into the pup's eyes, too; they should be bright and full of life.

When purchasing a poodle puppy, buyers hear from breeders that these dogs are just like any other puppy — times 10! They are very smart, stubborn and often have their own agendas. If a prospective owner isn't willing to spend a fair amount of time with a poodle, then the breed is not for them. A poodle wants to be with people more than other dogs and is quite similar to a 7-year-old boy in the sense that he needs attention and consistent reinforcement for behavioral parameters. Once through adolescence, however, a Poodle is the best friend, guardian and companion a person or family could have.

PUPPY PARTICULARS

Here are signs to look for when picking a poodle puppy from a breeder. When in doubt, ask the breeder which puppy they think has the best personality and temperament to fit your lifestyle.

1. Look at the area where the puppies spend most of their time. It's fine if they play outdoors part of the day, but they should sleep indoors at night so they can interact with people and become accustomed to hearing ordinary household noises, like a vacuum cleaner or television. This builds a solid foundation for a well-socialized and secure poodle puppy. The puppies' area should be clean, well-lit, have fresh drinking water and interesting toys.

2. Sure, you're only buying one puppy, but make sure to see all of the puppies in the litter. By 5 weeks of age, healthy pups will begin playing with one another and should be lively and energetic. It's OK if they're asleep when you visit, but stay long enough to see them wake up. Once they're up, they shouldn't be lethargic or weak, as this may be a sign of illness.

3. Pups should be confident and eager to greet you. A poodle pup who is shy or fearful and stays in the corner may be sick or insecure. Although some introverted pups come out of their shells later on, many do not. These dogs will always be fearful as adults and are not good choices for an active, noisy family with or without children, or for people who have never had a dog before. They frighten easily and will require a tremendous amount of training and socialization in order to live a happy life.

Choose a puppy who is happy and eager to interact with you but reject the one who is either too shy or too bossy. These temperament types are a challenge to deal with, and require a tremendous amount of training to socialize. The perfect poodle puppy personality is somewhere between the two extremes.

4. If it's feeding time during your visit, all pups should be eager to gobble up their food. A puppy refusing to eat may signal illness.

5. The dog's skin should be smooth, clean and shiny without any sores or bumps. Puppies should not be biting or scratching at themselves continuously, as this could signal fleas.

6. After 10 to 12 days, eyes should be open and clear without any redness or discharges. Pups should not be scratching at their eyes, as this may cause an infection or signal irritation.

7. Vomiting or coughing more than once is not normal. If so, a poodle puppy might be ill and should visit the veterinarian immediately.

8. Visit long enough to see the poodle pups eliminate. All stools should be firm without being watery or bloody.

These are signs of illness or that a puppy has worms.

9. Poodle puppies should walk or run freely without limping.

10. A healthy poodle puppy who is getting enough to eat should not be skinny. You should be able to slightly feel his ribs if you rub his abdomen, but you should not be able to see ribs protruding.

BREEDER PAPERS

Everything today comes with an instruction manual. When you purchase a poodle puppy, it's no different. A reputable breeder should give you a registration application; a sales contract; a health guarantee; your puppy's complete health records; a three-, four- or five-generation pedigree; and some general information on behavior, care, conformation, health and training.

Registration Application. This document from the AKC or UKC assigns your puppy a number and identifies the dog by listing his date of birth, the names of the parents and shows that he is registered as a purebred poodle. It doesn't prove whether or not your dog is a show- or a pet-quality poodle and doesn't provide any health guarantee.

Sales Contract. A reputable breeder should discuss the terms of the contract with you before asking you to sign it. This is a written understanding of both of your expectations and shows that the breeder cares about the pup's welfare throughout his life. The contract can include such terms as requiring you to keep the dog indoors at night, spaying or neutering if the puppy is not going to be a show dog, providing routine vet care and assurance that you'll feed your dog a healthy diet. Most responsible breeders will ask that you take your dog to obedience classes and earn a Canine Good Citizen title (an AKC training certification for dogs that exhibit good manners) before he is 2 years old. Many breeders also require new owners to have

---

Healthy Puppy Signs
Here are a few things you should look for when selecting a puppy from a litter.

1. **NOSE:** It should be slightly moist to the touch, but there shouldn't be excessive discharge. The puppy should not be sneezing or sniffling persistently.

2. **SKIN AND COAT:** Your poodle puppy's coat should be soft and shiny, without flakes or excessive shedding. Watch out for patches of missing hair, redness, bumps or sores. The pup should have a pleasant smell. Check for parasites, such as fleas or ticks.

3. **BEHAVIOR:** A healthy poodle puppy may be sleepy, but he should not be lethargic. A healthy puppy will be playful at times, not isolated in a corner. You should see occasional bursts of energy and interaction with littermates. When it's mealtime, a healthy puppy will take an interest in his food.

There are more signs to look for when picking out the perfect poodle puppy for your lifestyle. Download the list at **DogChannel.com/Club-Poodle**

totally secure fencing and gates around their yard. Poodles are incredible escape artists, and they will find a way out of the yard if there's even the slightest opening.

Health Guarantee. This includes a letter from a veterinarian that the puppy has been examined and is healthy, and states that the breeder will replace your dog if he were to develop a genetic, life-threatening illness during his lifetime.

Health Records. Here's everything you want to know about your puppy's and his parents' health. It should include the dates the puppy was vaccinated, dewormed and examined by a veterinarian for signs of heart murmur, plus the parents' test results for the presence or absence of hip and elbow dysplasia, heart problems and luxated patellas.

Pedigree. A breeder should provide new owners with a copy of the puppy's three-, four- or five-generation pedigree. Many breeders also have photos of the dog's ancestors that they will proudly share with you.

Extra Information. The best breeders pride themselves on handing over a notebook full of the latest information on poodle behavior, care, conformation, health and training. Be sure to read it

because it will provide valuable help while raising your poodle.

CHAPTER 4

HOME

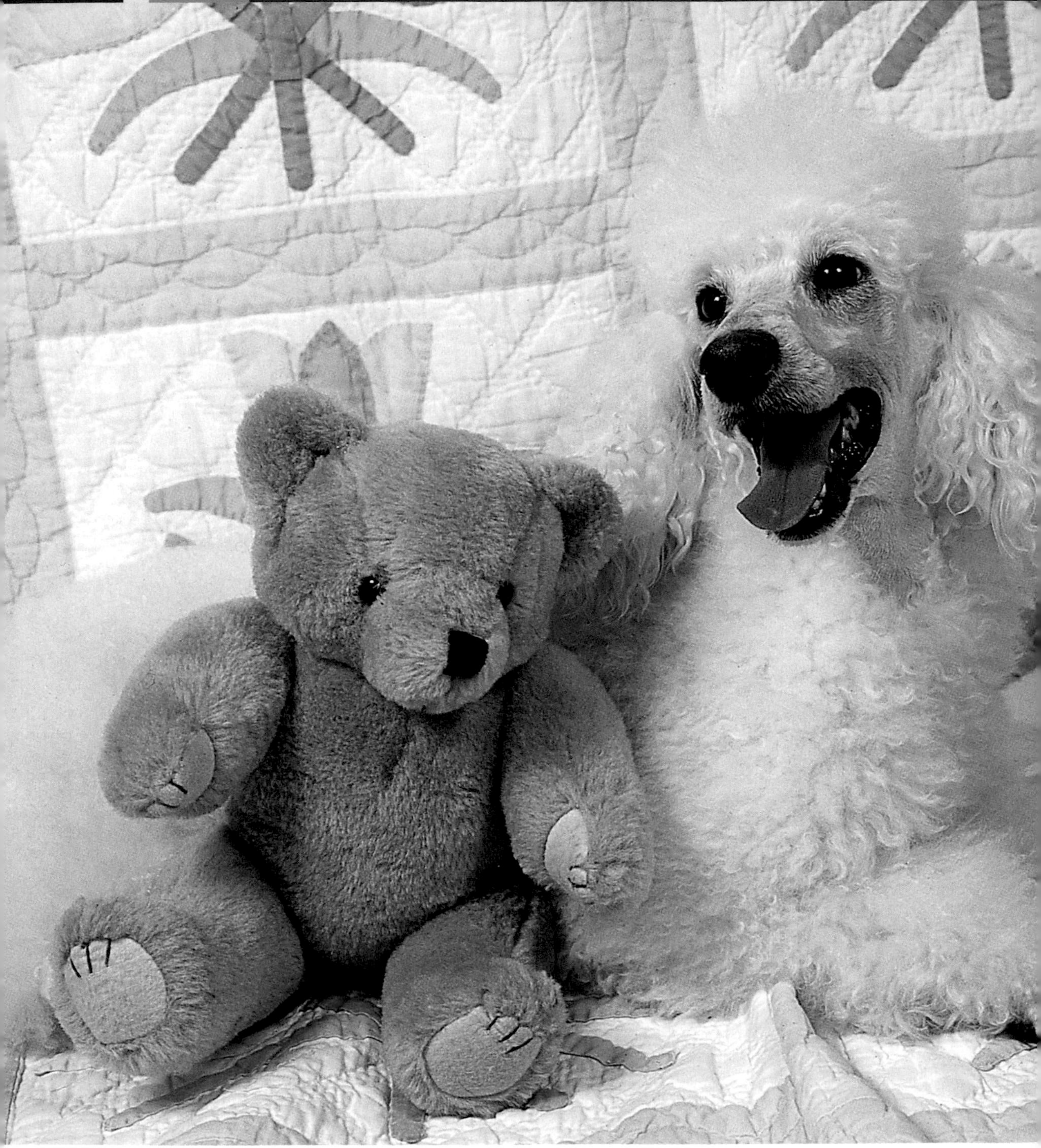

ESSENTIALS

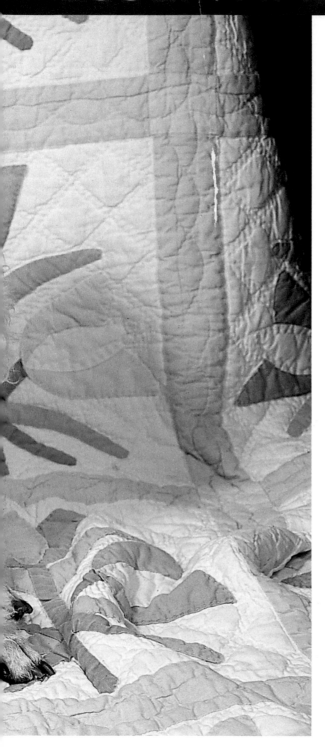

Don't for one second think that a poodle would prefer to live outside by the pool! He, like every other breed, wants to live with the best accommodations including plenty of toys, soft bedding and other "luxuries." Your home is now his home, too, and before you even bring that new puppy or rescue dog into his new forever home, be a smart owner and make your home accessible for him.

In fact, in order for him to grow into a stable, well-adjusted poodle, he has to feel comfortable in his surroundings. Remember, he is leaving the warmth and security of his mother and littermates, as well as the familiarity of the only place he has ever known, so it is important to make his transition to his new home as easy as possible.

PUPPY-PROOFING

Aside from making sure that your poodle will be comfortable in your home, you also have to ensure that your home is safe, which means taking the proper precautions to keep your pup away from things that are dangerous for him.

it's a Fact

Dangers lurk indoors and outdoors. Keep your curious poodle from investigating your shed and garage. Antifreeze and fertilizers, such as those you would use for roses, can kill any dog. Keep these items on high shelves that are out of reach.

A well-stocked toy box should contain three main categories of toys.

1. **action** — anything that you can throw or roll and get things moving
2. **distraction** — durable toys that make dogs work for a treat
3. **comfort** — soft, stuffed "security blankets"

Toys and accessories are great, but they can't replace what your poodle really craves: Your love and affection.

Puppy-proof your home inside and out before bringing your poodle home for the first time. Place breakables out of reach. If he is limited to certain places within the house, keep potentially dangerous items in off-limit areas. If your poodle is going to spend time in a crate, make sure that there isn't anything near it that he can reach if he sticks his curious little nose or paws through the openings.

The outside of your home must also be safe. Your pup will want to run and explore the yard, and he should be granted that freedom — as long as you are there to supervise. Do not let a fence give you a false sense of security; you would be surprised how crafty and persistent a poodle puppy can be in figuring out how to dig under a fence or squeeze his way through holes. The remedy is to thoroughly embed the fence into the ground. Be sure to repair or secure any gaps in the fence. Check the fence periodically to ensure that it is in good shape and make repairs as needed; a very determined puppy may work on the same spot until he is able to get through.

The following are a few common problem areas to watch out for in or around the home.

■ **Electrical cords and wiring:** No electrical cord or wiring is safe. Many office-supply stores sell products to keep wires gathered under computer desks, as well as products that prevent office chair wheels (and puppy teeth) from damaging electrical cords. If you have exposed cords and wires, these products aren't very expensive and can be used to keep a puppy out of trouble.

■ **Trash cans:** Don't waste your time trying to train your poodle not to get into the trash. Simply put the garbage behind a cabinet door and use a child-safe lock, if necessary. Dogs love bathroom trash,

Keeping your poodle puppy safe at home will allow him to become better adjusted.

which consists of items that can be extremely dangerous (i.e., cotton balls, cotton swabs, used razors, dental floss, etc.). Put the bathroom trash can in a cabinet under the sink and make sure you always shut the door to the bathroom.

■ **Household cleaners:** Make sure your poodle puppy doesn't have access to any of these deadly chemicals. Keep them behind closed cabinet doors, using child-safe locks, if necessary.

■ **Pest control sprays and poisons:** Chemicals to control ants or other pests should never be used in the house, if possible. Your poodle pup doesn't have to directly ingest these poisons to become ill; if he steps in the poison, he can experience toxic effects by licking his paws. Roach motels and other toxic pest traps are also yummy to dogs, so don't drop these behind couches or cabinets; if there's room for a roach motel, there's room for a determined poodle.

■ **Fabric:** Here's one you might not think about: Some puppies have a habit of licking blankets, upholstery, rugs or carpets. Though this habit seems fairly innocuous, over time the fibers from the upholstery or carpet can accumulate in the dog's stomach and cause a blockage. If you see your dog licking these items, remove the item or prevent him from having contact with it.

■ **Prescriptions, painkillers, supplements and vitamins:** Keep all medications in a cabinet. Also, be very careful when taking your prescription medications, supplements or vitamins: How often have you dropped a pill? You can be sure that your poodle puppy will be in between your legs and will snarf up the pill before you even start to say "No!" Dispense your own pills carefully without your poodle present.

■ **Miscellaneous loose items:** If it's not bolted to the floor, your puppy is likely to give the item a taste test. Socks, coins, children's toys, game pieces, cat toys — you name it. If it's on the floor, it's worth a try. Make sure the floors in your home are picked up and free of clutter.

FAMILY INTRODUCTIONS

Everyone in the house will be excited about the puppy's homecoming and will want to pet and play with him, but it is best to make the introduction low-key so as not to overwhelm your puppy. He already will be apprehensive. It is the first time he has been separated from his mother, littermates and breeder, and the ride to your home is likely to be the first time he has been in a car. The last thing you want to do is smother your poodle pup, as this will only frighten him further. This is not to say that human contact is unnecessary at this stage because this is the time when a connection between the pup and his human family is formed. Gentle petting and soothing words should help console your poodle, as well as letting him down to explore on his own (under your watchful eye, of course).

Your pup may approach the family members or may busy himself with exploring for a while. Gradually, each person should spend some time with the pup, one at a

JOIN OUR ONLINE Club Poodle™

Before you bring your poodle home, make sure you don't have anything that can put her in harm's way. Go to Club Poodle and download a list of poisonous plants and foods to avoid. Log on to **DogChannel.com/Club-Poodle** and click on "Downloads."

The first thing you should always do before your puppy comes home is to lie on the ground and look around. You want to be able to see everything your puppy is going to see. For the puppy, the world is one big chew toy.

— Cathleen Stamm, rescue volunteer in San Diego, Calif.

When you are unable to watch your poodle puppy, put her in a crate or an exercise pen on an easily cleanable floor. If she has an accident on carpeting, clean it completely and meticulously, so that it doesn't smell like her potty forever.

time, crouching down to get as close to the poodle's level as possible, letting him sniff their hands before petting him gently. He definitely needs human attention, and he needs to be touched; this is how to form an immediate bond. Just remember that the pup is experiencing a lot of things for the first time, all at once. There are new people, new noises, new smells and new things to investigate. Be gentle, be affectionate and be as comforting as you can possibly be.

PUP'S FIRST NIGHT HOME

You have traveled home with your new puppy safely in his crate. He may have already been to the vet for a thorough checkup — he's been weighed, his papers examined, perhaps he's even been vaccinated and dewormed as well. Your poodle has met and licked the whole family, including the excited children and the less-than-happy cat. He's explored his area, his new bed, the yard and everywhere else he's permitted. He's eaten his first meal at home and relieved himself in the proper place. Your poodle has heard lots of new sounds, smelled new friends and seen more of the outside world than ever before. This was just the first day! He's worn out and is ready for bed — or so you think!

Remember, this is your puppy's first night to sleep alone. His mother and littermates are no longer at paw's length, and he's scared, cold and lonely. Be reassuring to your new family member. This is not the time to spoil your poodle and give in to his inevitable whining.

Puppies whine. They whine to let others know where they are and hopefully to get company out of it. Place your poodle puppy in his new bed or crate in his room and close the door. Mercifully, he may fall asleep without a peep. If the inevitable occurs, ignore the whining; he is fine. Do not give in and visit your puppy. He will fall asleep eventually.

Many breeders recommend placing a piece of bedding from his former home in his new bed so that he will recognize the scent of his littermates. Others still advise placing a hot water bottle in his bed for warmth. The latter may be a good idea provided the pup doesn't attempt to suckle.

Your poodle's first night can be somewhat terrifying for him. Remember that you set the tone of nighttime at your house. Unless you want to play with your pup every night at 10 p.m., midnight and 2 a.m., don't initiate the habit. Your family will thank you, and so will your pup!

PET-SUPPLY STORE SHOPPING

It's fun shopping for new things for a new puppy. From training to feeding and sleeping to playing, your new poodle will need a few items to make life comfy, easy and fun. Be prepared and visit your local pet-supply store before you bring home your new family member.

◆ **Collar and ID tag:** Accustom your dog to wearing a collar the first day you bring him home. Not only will a collar and ID tag help your puppy in the event that he becomes lost, but collars are also an important training tool. If your poodle gets into

Smart owners will prepare
their homes for their new
dog's arrival, so he'll feel right
at home right off the bat.

9-1-1! If you don't know whether the plant, food or "stuff" your poodle just ate is toxic to dogs, call the ASPCA's Animal Poison Control Center (888-426-4435). Be prepared to provide your puppy's age and weight, her symptoms — if any — and how much of the plant, chemical, or substance she ingested, as well as how long ago you think she came into contact with the substance. The ASPCA charges a consultation fee for this service.

trouble, the collar will act as a handle, helping you divert him to a more appropriate behavior. Make sure the collar fits snugly enough so that your poodle cannot wriggle out of it, but is loose enough so that it will not be uncomfortably tight around his neck. You should be able to fit a finger between your pup's neck and the collar. Collars come in many styles, but for starting out, a simple buckle collar with an easy-release snap works great.

◆ **Leash:** For training or just for taking a stroll down the street, a leash is your poodle's vehicle to explore the outside world. Like collars, leashes come in a variety of styles and materials. A 6-foot nylon leash is a popular choice because it is lightweight and durable. As your pup grows and gets used to walking on the leash, you may want to purchase a flexible leash. These leads allow you to extend the length to give your dog a broader area to explore or to shorten the length to keep your dog closer to you.

◆ **Bowls:** Your dog will need two bowls: one for water and one for food. You may want two sets of bowls, one for inside and one for outside, depending on where your dog will be fed and where he will be spending time. Bowls should be sturdy enough so that they don't tip over easily. (Most have reinforced bottoms that prevent tipping.) Bowls usually are made of metal, ceramic or plastic, and should be easy to clean.

◆ **Crate:** A multipurpose crate serves as a bed, housetraining tool and travel carrier. It also is the ideal doggie den — a bedroom of sorts — that your poodle can retire to when he wants to rest or just needs a break. The crate should be large enough for your dog to stand in, turn around and lie down. You don't want any more room than this — especially if you're planning on using the crate to housetrain your dog — because he will eliminate in one corner and lie down in another. Get a crate that is big enough for your dog when he is an adult, and use dividers to limit the space when he's a puppy.

◆ **Bed:** Providing a soft, comfy bed for a growing poodle puppy brings about the risk that he'll rip it up and swallow pieces that could cause choking or blockage. That said, if your puppy seems the soft-bed, snuggle-bunny type, consider a few things to help save your purchase from being torn apart. For instance, some companies sell chew-resistant beds made of extra tough material with unexposed seams that thwart all but the most avid chewers. Flat beds consisting of two thick pieces of fabric sewn together without stuffing prove less tempting than de-stuffable beds.

If you are still worried that your puppy will chew the bedding in his crate, place safe chew and interactive toys within the crate to provide him more constructive pastime to satisfy his need to chew. Rotate these to maintain interest. If at any time you see your puppy start chewing on his

NOTABLE & QUOTABLE

Playing with toys from puppyhood encourages good behavior and social skills throughout your dog's life. A happy, playful dog is a content and well-adjusted one. Also, because all puppies chew to soothe their gums and help loosen puppy teeth, dogs should always have easy access to several different toys.

— dog trainer and author Harrison Forbes of Savannah, Tenn.

bed, say "*ah–ah*" and redirect his attention toward a suitable toy.

As time goes on and your maturing puppy calms down, you can buy all the neat, fluffy beds you want.

◆ **Gate:** Similar to those used for toddlers, gates help keep your poodle confined to one room or area when you can't supervise him. They also work to keep your dog out of areas you don't want him in.

Gates are available in many styles. Make sure you choose one with openings small enough so your puppy can't squeeze through the bars or any gaps.

◆ **Cleaning supplies:** Until your poodle puppy is housetrained, you will be doing a

SMART TIP!

Keep a crate in your vehi-cle and take your poodle along when you visit the drive-thru at the bank or your favorite fast-food restaurant. She can watch interactions, hear interesting sounds and maybe even earn a dog treat.

lot of cleaning. Accidents will occur, which is acceptable in the beginning because your puppy doesn't know any better. All you can do is be prepared to clean up any accidents. Old rags, towels, newspapers and a stain-and-odor remover are good to have on hand.

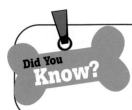
Everyone who rides in your car has to buckle up — even your poodle! Your dog can travel in the car inside her crate or you can use a doggie seat belt. These look like harnesses that attach to your car's seat-belt system.

◆ **Toys:** Today, your toy selection is almost unlimited. There are chew toys, stuffed toys, rubber toys, squeaky toys and interactive toys.

For teething puppies, chew toys provide a gum-soothing workout that helps keep those sharp teeth off your coffee table. Types vary from those chewed away in one or two sittings to others that last weeks or months. Though both are beneficial, as your poodle grows and his jaw strength increases, edible chew toys sometimes become barely more than a snack.

Most puppies love soft stuffed toys, some choosing a favorite to carry around and cuddle. Other puppies love tearing these toys apart! A smart owner will be mindful of the danger that the puppy might ingest parts of the stuffing or fabric and suffer an internal blockage.

Rubber toys present a sturdy yet soft option that many puppies enjoy chewing, chasing and fetching. Unless you own a Standard Poodle puppy with particularly strong jaws, quality rubber toys can usually be left safely with your poodle. Note: Never give your puppy a rubber toy small enough for him to swallow. The slippery surface slides down far too easily and makes it impossible to remove.

Squeaky toys come in countless shapes, forms and materials. Often useful as a training motivator, these toys have a major drawback. Many puppies and dogs become obsessed about "killing" the squeaker and often succeed by ripping the toy apart. The danger is that your poodle could swallow

Funny Bone

To err is human; to forgive, canine.

— *Anonymous*

the ripped pieces, causing a choking hazard or a potential intestinal blockage. Be sure to always supervise your dog's playtime with these toys.

Innovative and invaluable when raising a lively puppy, interactive toys help to keep your dog busy, develop his mind and burn off energy. With most interactive toys, your puppy extracts treats by licking them out, rolling the toy or playing with it. This self-reward system maintains interest until the goodies are gone.

Your poodle might also like to chase and catch balls that roll and bounce. The kind of balls you should buy will depend on you and your dog's preferences. Just keep in mind that many dogs die each year from choking on a ball. Replace them as your poodle grows, so that they'll always be the appropriate size for his mouth and throat.

BEYOND THE BASICS

The basic items discussed previously are the bare necessities. You will find out what else you and your new dog need as you go along — grooming supplies, flea/tick protection — and these things will vary depending on your situation. It is important, however, that you have everything you need to make your poodle comfortable in his new home.

Some ordinary household items make great toys for your poodle — as long you make sure they are safe. Tennis balls, plastic water bottles, old towels and more can be transformed into fun with a little creativity. You can find a list of homemade toys at **DogChannel.com/Club-Poodle**

HOUSETRAINING

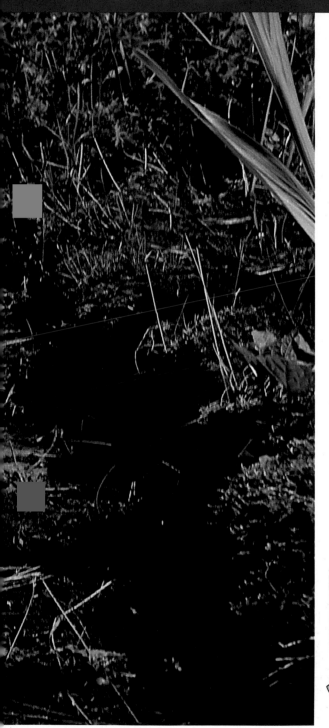

U nexciting as it may be, the house-training part of puppy rearing greatly affects the budding relationship between a smart owner and his puppy — particularly when it becomes an area of ongoing contention. Fortunately, armed with suitable knowledge, patience and common sense, you'll find housetraining progresses at a relatively smooth rate. This leaves more time for the important things, like cuddling your adorable puppy, showing him off and laughing at his high jinks.

The keys to successful housetraining are total supervision and management — crates, tethers, exercise pens and leashes — until you know your dog has developed preferences for outside surfaces (grass, gravel, concrete) instead of carpet, tile or hardwood, and knows that potty happens outside.

IN THE BEGINNING

For the first two to three weeks of a puppy's life, his mother helps the pup to eliminate. The mother also keeps the whelping box or "nest area" clean. When pups begin to walk around and eat on their own, they choose where they eliminate. You can train your puppy to relieve himself wherever

it's a Fact Ongoing housetraining difficulties may indicate your pup has a health problem, warranting a vet check. A urinary infection, parasites, a virus and other nasty issues greatly affect your puppy's ability to hold pee or poop.

Properly cleaning accidents with an enzyme solution will dramatically reduce the time it takes to housetrain your poodle because she won't be drawn back to the same areas to eliminate.

you choose, but this must be somewhere suitable. You should bear in mind from the outset that when your puppy is old enough to go out in public places, you must be considerate and pick up after him. You will always have to carry with you a small plastic bag or poop scoop.

Outdoor training includes such surfaces as grass, soil and concrete. Indoor training usually means training your dog on newspaper. When deciding on the surface and location that you will want your poodle to use, be sure it is going to be permanent. Training your dog on grass and then changing two months later to dirt or concrete is extremely difficult for dog as well as owner.

Next, choose the cue you will use each and every time you want your puppy to eliminate. "Let's go," "hurry up" and "potty" are examples of cues commonly used by smart dog owners.

Get in the habit of giving your puppy the chosen relief cue before you take him out. That way, when he becomes an adult, you will be able to determine if he wants to go out when you ask him. A confirmation will be signs of interest, such as wagging his tail, watching you intently or going to the door.

LET'S START WITH THE CRATE

Clean animals by nature, dogs dislike soiling where they sleep and eat. This fact makes a crate a useful tool for housetraining. When purchasing a new crate, consider that

an appropriately sized crate will allow adequate room for an adult dog to stand full-height, lie on his side without scrunching and turn around easily. If debating plastic versus wire crates, short-haired breeds sometimes prefer the warmer, draft-blocking quality of plastic, while furry dogs often like the cooling airflow of a wire crate.

Some crates come with a movable wall that reduces the interior size to provide enough space for your puppy to stand, turn and lie down, while not allowing him room to soil one end and sleep in the other. The problem is that if your puppy goes potty in the crate anyway, the divider forces him to lie in his own excrement.

This can work against you by desensitizing your puppy against his normal, instinctive revulsion to resting where he has just eliminated. If scheduling permits you or a responsible family member to clean the crate soon after it's soiled, then you can continue to cratetrain because limiting crate size does encourage your puppy to hold it. Otherwise, give him enough room to move away from an unclean area until he's better able to control his elimination.

Needless to say, not every poodle puppy adheres to this guideline. If your poodle moves along at a faster pace, thank your lucky stars. Should he progress slower, accept it and remind yourself that he'll improve. Be aware that puppies frequently hold it longer at night than during the day. Just because your puppy sleeps for six or more hours through the night does not mean he can hold it that long during the more active daytime hours.

One last bit of advice on the crate: Place it in the corner of a high-traffic room, such as the family room or kitchen. Social and curious by nature, dogs like to feel included in family happenings. Creating a quiet

In addition to house-training, crates are useful for travel.

Housetraining shouldn't cause excess stress and anxiety, but your puppy still won't be 100 percent accident free. No pup is perfect.

retreat by putting the crate in an unused area may seem like a good idea, but results in your puppy feeling insecure and isolated. Watching his people pop in and out of the crate room reassures your puppy that he's not forgotten.

A PUP'S GOT NEEDS

Your puppy needs to relieve himself after play periods, after each meal, after he has been sleeping and any time he indicates that he is looking for a place to urinate or defecate.

The urinary and intestinal tract muscles of very young puppies are not fully developed. Therefore, like human babies, puppies need to relieve themselves frequently. Take your puppy out often — every hour for an 8-week-old, for example — and always immediately after sleeping and eating. The older the puppy, the less often he will need to relieve himself. Finally, as a mature, healthy adult, he will require only three to five relief trips per day.

HOUSING HELPS

Because the types of housing and control you provide for your poodle puppy have a direct relationship on the success of housetraining, you must consider the various aspects of both before beginning training. Taking a new puppy home and turning him loose in your house can be compared to turning a child loose in a sports arena and telling the child that the place is all his! The

How often does a poodle puppy do her business? A lot! Go to **DogChannel.com/Club-Poodle** and download the typical peeing and pooping schedule of a puppy. You can also download a chart that you can fill out to track your dog's elimination timetable, which will help you with housetraining.

JOIN OUR ONLINE
Club Poodle™

A positive approach to house-training includes praise and rewards when the task is accomplished correctly.

NOTABLE & QUOTABLE

Reward your pup with a high-value treat immediately after he potties to reinforce going in the proper location, then play for a short time afterward. This teaches that good things happen after pottying outside! — Victoria Schade, certified pet dog trainer, from Annandale, Va.

sheer enormity of the place would be too much for him to handle. Instead, offer the puppy clearly defined areas where he can play, sleep, eat and live. A room of the house where the family gathers is the most obvious choice.

Puppies are social animals and need to feel like they are a part of the pack right from the start. Hearing your voice, watching you while you are doing things and smelling you nearby are all positive reinforcers that he is now a member of your pack. Usually a family room, the kitchen or a nearby adjoining breakfast area is ideal for providing safety and security for puppy and owner.

Within that room, there should be a smaller area that your poodle puppy can call his own. An alcove, a wire or fiberglass dog crate, or a fenced (not boarded!) corner from which he can view the activities of his new family will be fine. The designated area should be lined with clean bedding and a toy. Water must always be available, in a nonspill container, once your dog is housetrained.

IN CONTROL

By control, we mean helping the puppy to create a lifestyle pattern that will be compatible to that of his human pack (you!). Just as we guide our children to learn our way of life, we must show our poodle pup when it is time to play, eat, sleep, exercise and entertain himself.

Your puppy should always sleep in his crate. He should also learn that during times of household confusion and excessive activity, such as at breakfast when family members are preparing for the day, he can play by himself in relative safety and comfort in his designated area. Each time you leave your poodle alone, he should understand exactly where he is supposed to stay.

Puppies are chewers. They cannot tell the difference between lamp cords, television wires, shoes or table legs. Chewing into a television wire, for example, can be fatal to the puppy, while a shorted wire can start a fire in the house.

If the puppy chews on the arm of the chair when he is alone, don't discipline him angrily when you get home. This will only make him think that your coming home means he is going to be punished. (He will not remember chewing the chair and is incapable of making the association of the discipline with his naughty deed.)

Other times of excitement, such as family parties, can be fun for your puppy, provided that he can view the activities from the security of his designated area. This way, he is not underfoot, and he is not

being fed all sorts of tidbits that will probably cause him stomach distress, yet he
still feels a part of the fun.

SCHEDULE A SOLUTION

A puppy should be taken to his relief
area each time he is released from his designated area, after meals, after play sessions and when he first awak-
ens in the morning (at 8 weeks
of age, this can mean 5 a.m.!).
Your puppy will indicate that
he's ready "to go" by circling or
sniffing busily — do not misinterpret these signs. For a puppy
less than 10 weeks of age, a
routine of taking him out every
hour is necessary. As your
puppy grows, he will be able to
wait for longer periods of time.

Keep potty trips to your
puppy's relief area short. Stay
no more than 5 or 6 minutes,
and then return to inside the
house. If your puppy potties
during that time, lavishly praise
him and then immediately take
him indoors. If he does not
potty, but he has an accident
later when you go back indoors,
pick him up, say "No!" and
return to his relief area. Wait a
few minutes, then return to the
house again. Never hit your
poodle puppy or rub his face in
urine or excrement when he
has had an accident.

Once indoors, put your puppy
in his crate until you have had
time to clean up his accident.
Then release him to the family
area and watch him more
closely than before. Chances

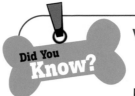

Did You Know?

White vinegar makes a good odor remover if you don't have any professional cleaners on hand; use one-quarter cup vinegar to one quart of water.

A housetrained poodle is a joy to take with you when you travel.

SMART TIP!

When proximity prevents you from going home at lunch or during periods when overtime crops up, make alternative arrangements for getting your puppy out. Hire a pet-sitting or walking service, or enlist the aid of an obliging neighbor.

are, his accident was a result of your not picking up his potty signals or waiting too long before offering him the opportunity to relieve himself. Never hold a grudge against your puppy for accidents.

Let your puppy learn that going outdoors means it is time to relieve himself, not to play. Once trained, he will be able to play indoors and outdoors and still differentiate between the times for play versus the times for relief.

Help him develop regular hours for naps, being alone, playing by himself and just resting — all in his crate. Encourage him to entertain himself while you are busy elsewhere. Let him learn that having you nearby is comforting, but it is not your main purpose in life to provide him with undivided attention.

Each time you put your poodle puppy in his own area, use the same cue, whatever

suits you best. Soon, he will run to his crate or special area when he hears you say those words. Remember that one of the primary ingredients in housetraining your poodle puppy is control. Regardless of your lifestyle, there will always be occasions when you will need to have a place where your dog can stay and be happy and safe. Cratetraining is the answer for now and in the future.

A few key elements are really all you need for a successful housetraining method: consistency, frequency, praise, control and supervision. By following these procedures with a normal, healthy puppy, you and your poodle will soon be past the stage of accidents and ready to move on to a full and rewarding life together.

it's a **Fact**

Canines are descendants of wolves. So think of your poodle's crate as a modern-day den. The cozy, confined space offers him a place of comfort and solitude.

10 HOUSETRAINING HOW-TOs

1. Decide where you want your poodle to eliminate. Take her there every time until she gets the idea. Pick a spot that's easy to access. Remember, puppies have very little time between "gotta go" and "oops."

2. Teach an elimination cue, such as "go potty" or "get busy." Say this every time you take your poodle to eliminate. Don't keep chanting the cue, just say it once or twice then keep quiet so you won't distract your dog.

3. Praise calmly when your dog eliminates, but stand there a little longer in case there's more.

4. Keep potty outings for potty only. Take the dog to the designated spot, tell her "go potty" and just stand there. If she needs to eliminate, she will do so within five minutes.

5. Don't punish for potty accidents; punishment can hinder progress. If you catch your poodle in the act indoors, verbally interrupt but don't scold. Gently carry or lead your pup to the approved spot, let her finish, then praise.

6. If it's too late to interrupt an accident, scoop the poop or blot up the urine afterward with a paper towel. Immediately take your dog and her deposit (gently!) to the potty area.

Place the poop or trace of urine on the ground and praise the pup. If she sniffs at her waste, praise more. Let your poodle know you're pleased when her waste is in the correct area.

7. Keep track of when and where your poodle eliminates — that will help you anticipate potty times. Regular meals mean regular elimination, so feed your dog scheduled, measured meals instead of free-feeding (leaving food available at all times).

8. Hang a bell on a sturdy cord from the doorknob. Before you open the door to take your puppy out for potty, shake the string and ring the bell. Most dogs soon realize the connection between the bell ringing and the door opening, then they'll try it out for themselves.

9. Dogs naturally return to re-soil where they've previously eliminated, so thoroughly clean up all accidents. Household cleaners usually will do the job, but special enzyme solutions may work better.

10. If the ground is littered with too much waste, your poodle may seek a cleaner place to eliminate. Scoop the potty area daily, leaving behind just one "reminder."

VET VISITS AND

CHAPTER
6

EVERYDAY CARE

Your selection of a veterinarian for your poodle should be based on personal recommendations of the doctor's skills, and, if possible, his experience with your poodle variety: Toy, Miniature or Standard. If the veterinarian is based nearby, it also will be helpful and more convenient because you might have an emergency or need to make multiple visits for treatments.

FIRST STEP: SELECT THE RIGHT VET

All licensed veterinarians are capable of dealing with routine medical issues such as infections and injuries, as well as the promotion of good health (like vaccinations). If the problem affecting your poodle is more complex, your vet may refer you to someone with more detailed knowledge of what is wrong. This usually will be a specialist such as a veterinary dermatologist or veterinary ophthalmologist.

Veterinary procedures are very costly and, as treatments improve, they are going to become more expensive. It is quite acceptable to discuss matters of cost with your vet; if there is more than one treatment option, cost may be a factor in deciding which route to take.

Smart owners will look for a veterinarian before they actually need one. For new pet owners, start looking for a veterinarian a month or two before you bring home your new poodle puppy. That will give you time to meet candidate veterinarians, check out the condition of the clinic, meet the staff and see who you feel most comfortable with. If you already have a poodle puppy, look sooner rather than later, preferably not in the midst of a veterinary health crisis.

Also, list the qualities that are important to you. Points to consider or investigate:

Convenience: Proximity to your home, extended hours or drop-off services are helpful for people who work regular business hours, have a busy schedule or don't want to drive far. If you have mobility issues, finding a vet who makes house calls or a service that provides pet transport might be particularly important.

Size: A one-person practice will ensure that you will always be dealing with the same vet during each and every visit. "That person can really get to know you and your dog," says Bernadine Cruz, D.V.M., of Laguna Hills Animal Hospital in Laguna Hills, Calif. The downside is that the sole practitioner does not have the immediate input of another vet, and if your vet becomes ill or takes time off, you may be out of luck.

A multiple-doctor practice offers consistency if your dog needs to come in unexpectedly on a day when your veterinarian isn't there. Additionally, your vet can quickly consult with his colleagues within the clinic if he's unsure about a diagnosis or a treatment.

If you find a veterinarian within that practice who you really like, you can make your appointments with that individual, establishing the same kind of bond that you would with the solo practitioner.

Appointment Policies: Some practices are by-appointment only, which could minimize your wait time. However, if a sudden problem arises with your poodle and the veterinarians are booked up, they might not be able to squeeze your pet in that day. Some clinics are walk-in only, which is great for impromptu or crisis visits, but without scheduling may involve longer waits to see the next available veterinarian. Some practices offer the best of both worlds by maintaining an appointment schedule but also keeping slots open throughout the day for walk-ins.

Basic vs. Full Service vs. State-of-the-Art: A veterinarian practice with high-tech equipment offers greater diagnostic capabilities and treatment options, important for tricky or difficult health cases. However, the cost of pricey equipment is passed along to the clients, so you could pay more for routine canine procedures — the bulk of most pets' appointments. Some practices offer boarding, grooming, training classes and other services on the premises — conveniences some pet owners appreciate.

Fees and Payment Polices: How much does a routine visit cost? If there is a significant price difference, be sure to ask why. If you intend to carry health insurance on your poodle or want to pay by credit card, check that the clinic accepts those payment options.

FIRST VET VISIT

It is much easier, less costly and more effective to practice preventive medicine than to fight bouts of illness and disease. Properly bred puppies of all breeds come from parents who were selected based upon their genetic disease profile. The puppies' mother should have been vaccinated, free of all internal and external parasites and properly nourished. For these reasons, a visit to the veterinarian who cared for the mother is recommended if at all possible. The mother passes disease resistance to her puppies, which should last from 8 to 10 weeks. Unfortunately, she can also pass on parasites and infection. This is why knowing about her health is useful in learning more about the health of her puppies.

Now that you have your poodle puppy home safe and sound, it's time to arrange your puppy's first trip to the veterinarian. Perhaps your poodle's breeder can recommend someone in the area who specializes in poodles, or maybe you know other poodle owners who can suggest a good vet. Either way, you should make an appointment within a couple of days of bringing home your puppy. If possible, see if you can

Talk to your neighbors about the vet they've chosen for their dogs and other animals. Word of mouth is a great way to find a good local vet.

stop for this first veterinarian appointment before going home.

The pup's first vet visit will consist of an overall examination to make sure that your pup does not have any problems that are not apparent to you. The veterinarian will also set up a schedule for the pup's vaccinations; the breeder should inform you of which ones your puppy has already received, and the vet can continue from there.

Your puppy also will have his teeth examined and have his skeletal conformation and general health checked by the veterinarian prior to certification. Puppies in certain breeds have problems with their kneecaps, cataracts and other eye problems, heart murmurs and undescended testicles. They may also have behavioral problems, which your veterinarian can evaluate if he or she has had relevant training.

VACCINATION SCHEDULING

Most vaccinations are given by injection and should only be given by a veterinarian. Both you and the vet should keep a record of the date of the injection, the identification of the vaccine and the amount given. Some vets give a first vaccination at 8 weeks of age, but most breeders prefer the course not to commence until about 10 weeks because of interaction with the antibodies produced by the mother. The vaccination scheduling is usually based on a 15-day cycle. You should take your vet's advice as to when to vaccinate, as this may differ according to the vaccine used.

The usual vaccines contain immunizing doses of several different viruses such as distemper, parvovirus, parainfluenza and hepatitis. There are other vaccines available when the puppy is at a greater risk for viral exposures. You should rely on your vet's advice. This is especially true for the booster immunizations. Most vaccination programs require a booster when the puppy is a year old and once a year thereafter. In some cases, circumstances may require more frequent immunizations.

Kennel cough, more formally known as *tracheobronchitis*, is combatted with a vac-

Set up a vet visit before you even bring your new dog home, so you can interview the veterinary staff.

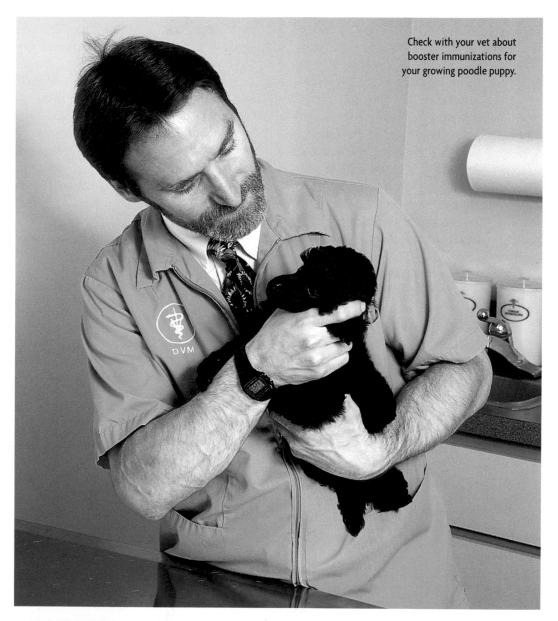

Check with your vet about booster immunizations for your growing poodle puppy.

Misha is a very sweet dog. He loves to be held and to cuddle; he will fall asleep right in my lap. He is also very smart. Misha is not afraid of water. He will try to go in the ocean even if the waves are big. One time he tried to 'rescue' me from the ocean but ended up having to be rescued himself.
— *Toy Poodle owner Dina Kleiman of Laguna Niguel, Calif.*

cine that is sprayed into the dog's nostrils. Kennel cough is usually included in routine vaccinations, but it is often not as effective as the vaccines for other major diseases.

Your veterinarian will probably recommend that your poodle puppy be fully vaccinated before you take him on outings. There are airborne diseases, parasite eggs in the grass and unexpected visits from other dogs that might be dangerous to your puppy's health. Other dogs are the most harmful reservoir of pathogenic organisms, as everything they have can be transmitted to your puppy.

6 Months to 1 Year of Age: Unless you intend to breed or show your dog, neutering or spaying your poodle at 6 months of age is recommended. Discuss this with your veterinarian. Neutering and spaying have proven to be beneficial to male and female puppies, respectively. Besides eliminating the possibility of pregnancy, it inhibits (but does not prevent) breast cancer in females and prostate cancer in male dogs.

Your veterinarian should provide your puppy with a thorough dental evaluation at 6 months of age, ascertaining whether all his permanent teeth have erupted prop-

erly. A home dental care regimen should be initiated at 6 months, including weekly brushing and providing good dental devices (such as nylon bones). Regular dental care promotes healthy teeth, fresh breath and a longer life.

Dogs Older Than 1 Year: Continue to visit the veterinarian at least once a year as bodily functions do change with age. The eyes and ears are no longer as efficient. Liver, kidney and intestinal functions often decline. Proper dietary changes recommended by your veterinarian can make life more pleasant for your aging poodle and you.

EVERYDAY HAPPENINGS

Keeping your poodle healthy is a matter of keen observation and quick action when necessary. Knowing what's normal for your dog will help you recognize signs of trouble before they blossom into a full-blown emergency situation.

Even if the problem is minor, such as a cut or scrape, you'll want to care for it immediately to prevent infection, as well as

Smart owners won't pick just any vet out of the phone book; they will invest time in researching and interviewing the best vet for their dog.

to ensure that your dog doesn't make it worse by chewing or scratching at it. Here's what to do for common, minor injuries or illnesses, and how to recognize and deal with emergencies.

Cuts and Scrapes: For a cut or scrape that's half an inch or smaller, clean the wound with saline solution or warm water and use tweezers to remove any splinters or other debris. Apply an antibiotic ointment. No bandage is necessary unless the wound is on a paw, which can pick up dirt when your dog walks on it. Deep cuts with lots of bleeding or those caused by glass or some other object should be treated by your veterinarian.

Cold Symptoms: Dogs don't actually get colds, but they can get illnesses that have similar symptoms, such as coughing, a runny nose or sneezing. Dogs cough for any number of reasons, from respiratory infections to inhaled irritants to congestive heart failure. Take your poodle to the veterinarian for prolonged coughing, or coughing accompanied by labored breathing, runny eyes and nose or bloody phlegm.

A runny nose that continues for more than several hours requires veterinary attention, as well. If your poodle sneezes, he may have some mild nasal irritation that will resolve on its own, but frequent sneezing, especially if it's accompanied by a runny nose, may indicate anything from allergies to an infection or something stuck in his nose.

Vomiting and Diarrhea: Sometimes dogs can suffer minor gastric upset when they eat a new type of food, eat too much, eat the contents of the trash can or become excited or anxious. Give your poodle's stomach

An active dog lives a longer and happier life.

a rest by withholding food for 12 hours, and then feeding him a bland diet such as rice and chicken, gradually returning your dog to his normal food. Projectile vomiting or vomiting or diarrhea that continues for more than 48 hours is another matter. If this happens, immediately take your poodle to the veterinarian.

MORE HEALTH HINTS

A poodle's anal glands can cause problems if not periodically evacuated. In the wild, dogs regularly clear their anal glands to mark their territory. In domestic dogs this function is no longer necessary; thus, their contents can build up and clog, causing discomfort. Signs that the anal glands — located on both sides of the anus — need emptying are if a poodle drags his rear end along the ground or keeps turning around to lick the area of discomfort.

While care must be taken not to cause injury, anal glands can be evacuated by pressing gently on either side of the anal

Just like with infants, puppies need a series of vaccinations to ensure that they stay healthy during their first year of life. Download a vaccination chart from **DogChannel.com/Club-Poodle** that you can fill out for your poodle.

I love my poodle because when I look into Baxter's eyes, I see all the love, loyalty and trust he has for me. When looking back at me, I'm confident he is safe and secure knowing that his love will be returned, his loyalty will be honored and his trust will never be betrayed. What a joy!

— poodle owner Powers Smith of Charleston, W.V.

opening and by using a piece of cotton or a tissue to collect the foul-smelling matter. If anal glands are allowed to become impacted, abscesses can form, causing pain and the need for veterinary attention.

Poodles can get into all sorts of mischief, so it is not uncommon for them to swallow something poisonous in the course of their investigations. Obviously, an urgent visit to the vet is required under such circumstances, but if possible, when you call your vet, inform him which poisonous substance has been ingested, because different treatments are needed. Should it be necessary to cause your dog to vomit (which is not always the case with poisoning), a small lump of baking soda, given orally, will have an immediate effect. Alternatively, a small teaspoon of salt or mustard, dissolved in water, will have a similar effect but may be more difficult to administer and take longer to work.

Did You Know?

Obesity is linked to the earlier onset of age-related health problems. Keep weight in line by providing sufficient exercise and play and by feeding proper serving sizes. Because calorie requirements decline as your puppy reaches adulthood, and can drop 25 to 30 percent within a couple of months after spaying/neutering, you'll probably need to reduce serving portions and switch to a less calorie-dense diet.

Puppies often have painful fits while they are teething. These are not usually serious and are brief. Of course, you must be certain that the cause is nothing more than teething. Giving a puppy something hard to chew on usually will solve this temporary problem.

Choose a vet before you choose your poodle puppy, so you can be ready from day one, if an emergency occurs.

No matter how careful you are with your precious poodle, sometimes unexpected injuries happen. Be prepared for an emergency by creating a canine first-aid kit. Find out what essentials you need on **DogChannel.com/Club-Poodle** — just click on "Downloads."

Toy, Miniature and Standard Poodles by-and-large are intelligent, healthy and long-lived animals. But as with any species or breed of animal, despite good care, health problems can sometimes arise. In the three varieties of poodles, some of the disorders occasionally seen include idiopathic epilepsy, progressive retinal atrophy, *sebaceous adenitis* and Addison's disease.

Although chances are you won't see any of these problems befall your pet, it's important to be aware of the health concerns that involve your breed.

EPILEPSY

Idiopathic epilepsy is a disorder associated with recurrent seizures that aren't a consequence of other disorders (head trauma, low blood sugar, poisoning, heart disease, kidney or liver failure, or electrolyte imbalances). Seen in dozens of different dog breeds, idiopathic epilepsy is one of the most common diseases of the nervous system in dogs. It is, however, difficult to diagnose because seizures can occur for several reasons, and there is no actual epilepsy test. Hence, the diagnosis is actually made by eliminating other possible causes — an exclusion diagnosis.

Did You Know?

Dogs can get many diseases from ticks, including Lyme disease, Rocky Mountain spotted fever, tick bite paralysis and many others.

"The onset of idiopathic epilepsy generally occurs between the ages of 1 and 5 years," says Steven Zinderman, D.V.M., medical director at Roadside Veterinary Clinic in Highland, Mich. "Typical seizures are called tonic-clonic (grand-mal) seizures. The dog may stiffen and fall over with his legs extended, neck arched and head thrown back. He may vocalize, lose control of his bowel and urinary functions, and drool excessively; this is the tonic phase and could last up to 30 seconds.

"The clonic phase follows, during which the dog may paddle his legs as if running, have facial and muscle twitches, and chomp his jaws; this could last another 60 seconds. During the whole process, the dog is unconscious and could have irregular breathing. However, his breathing returns to normal once the seizure ends."

To obtain a diagnosis, your veterinarian will runs several tests — bloodwork, urinalysis, toxin scan and liver and thyroid function tests — to pinpoint or rule out other causes. Your veterinarian may also refer your dog to a veterinary neurologist for an MRI or CT scan of the brain, an analysis of spinal fluid and an electroencephalogram.

Although there is no cure for idiopathic epilepsy, in most cases the disease can be managed. "The most common drugs used to treat epilepsy are the antiseizure drugs phenobarbital and potassium bromide," Zinderman says. "These are sometimes used in combination and must be adjusted for each individual patient. Some medications may make your pet drowsy, but this should not restrict his activity. However, not all patients are treated with medication: If your dog's seizures are mild and

don't occur more than once every few months, treatment may not be necessary."

If your dog is prescribed antiseizure medicine, keep an accurate record of any seizures that still occur (the date and how long they lasted) and have your dog's blood levels tested periodically (per your veterinarian's recommendation) in order to measure the concentration of medication in your dog's blood and to avoid any adverse side effects from the medication. "This will help manage the disease," Zinderman says. Depending upon how your dog responds, medication adjustments may be needed in order to find the appropriate drug and dosage that works best for your pet.

Despite medication, your dog may still have seizure activity. You can take several steps during a seizure to see to your dog's comfort and safety. "Your dog won't be in danger of swallowing his tongue, so don't put your hands near his mouth, because you may be bit if jaw chomping begins," Zinderman warns. "To prevent injury, make sure your dog isn't near stairs, sharp objects or water. Put a pillow under his head to protect him and move other pets away from the seizing dog because they may become frightened. If the seizure lasts longer than four to five minutes, or more than one seizure occurs in a day, see your veterinarian immediately.

"With idiopathic epilepsy, seizures may occur on a fairly regular basis, then suddenly change in frequency and duration," Zinderman adds. "Seizures can also occur due to stress in the animal's environment or even changes in the weather. The one thing certain with seizures is that they're unpredictable."

Maggie, an energetic poodle who happens to have epilepsy, takes twice-daily doses of phenobarbital to control her symp-

toms. Initially, she was prescribed a lower dose, but after her seizure activity continued — usually in a cluster of two to five episodes within a 24-hour period — Maggie's veterinarian gradually increased the dosage. "I also give Maggie oral diazepam for several days after the seizure episodes, which acts as a preventive," owner Ellen Krieger of Manalapan, N.J. says.

Krieger also made a few dietary changes based on information she received at the Canine Epilepsy Resource Center (www.canine-epilepsy.com), a website for owners of epileptic dogs. The site contains articles written by several veterinary researchers and experts. "I also had Maggie's thyroid tested based on advice from the epilepsy website and found she had an underactive thyroid, which can contribute to seizures," Krieger says.

Maggie is still playful but is also equally content to relax on the front porch and watch the world go by. "She loves furry, squeaky toys and her dog biscuits," Krieger says, "and will sneak in cat food and treats whenever possible!"

SMART TIP! **Many canine skin irritations can be reduced or simply avoided by employing a simple preventive regimen:**

- Keep your poodle's skin clean and dry.
- Shampoo your dog regularly (especially during allergy season) with a hypoallergenic shampoo.
- Rinse the coat thoroughly.
- Practice good flea control.
- Supplement your dog's diet with fatty acids, such as omega-3.

Maggie is now less troubled by seizures, although they haven't completely subsided. "We've given up extended vacations because we don't feel right leaving her for more than a day or two," Krieger reports. "We live with a time schedule that revolves around her medications. However, we wouldn't trade one minute of our time with her for anything in the world!"

GOING BLIND

Having a dog that can go blind is a scary experience, and unfortunately, Toy and Miniature Poodles can be affected by a vision-robbing disorder called progressive retinal atrophy.

"PRA refers to a group of inherited disorders that cause degeneration of the retina," explains Lila Miller, D.V.M., senior director and veterinary advisor for the American Society for the Prevention of Cruelty to Animals. "It can occur after the retina matures or before the retina develops at 12 weeks of age; affects both eyes; and ultimately results in total blindness." Although affected Toys and Miniatures generally start displaying signs of vision problems between the ages of 3 and 5 years, PRA rarely affects Standard Poodles.

The first indication of PRA is hesitation in your dog to go out at night or difficulty negotiating his way in dim lighting. "Clinical signs of PRA often start with night blindness and gradually progress to the point where it's difficult to see even in bright light," Miller says. "The blindness may seem to have a sudden onset, but this is usually not the case. The pupils will be dilated more than usual at night and the eyes may seem more reflective."

Although your veterinarian can make a preliminary diagnosis based on your dog's history and clinical signs, such as

Buying your poodle from a responsible breeder greatly reduces the chances of genetic health issues.

increased pupil dilation and an unusual shine in the eyes, it requires advanced training and specialty equipment to evaluate the retinal changes and make a definitive PRA diagnosis.

There is no cure or treatment for PRA. "However, vision loss is gradual and non-painful, and most dogs learn to adapt to their surroundings," Miller emphasizes. "Owners can help by keeping their dogs on a leash when outdoors, maintaining the same routine and keeping furniture, food and water dishes in the same place."

Paul Owens, certified evaluator for The Delta Society's Animal Assisted Therapy Program, notes that blind dogs can learn to get along well in spite of the physical challenge. "Teaching a blind dog to navigate safely is simple," Owens says. "Dogs remember scents and substrates, so if you slowly walk a dog around and let him investigate, he will remember the route after numerous repetitions by utilizing his senses of smell and touch."

Owens, owns a Portuguese Water Dog that has been blind since was 9 years of age. He suggests highlighting the pathway leading to and from your home with a scent, such as your perfume or cologne, and "laying a track" with droplets leading to the entry; this can help your dog find his way. "You can also leave an old T-shirt with your scent near the entry to help orientation," he says.

"Teach your blind dog to go up or down steps by teaching it key phrases, such as 'be careful' or 'go slow,' whenever he gets close to an obstacle, such as a wall or steps," suggests Owens, who is a member of the National Association of Dog Obedience Instructors and the Association of Pet Dog Trainers. "This can be done safely by leading him around on a leash and guiding his movement. Then you can teach your dog to either 'turn left' or 'right' or 'go around,' or even to put its paw out to step up or down by saying 'step.'

"While the dog is learning these signals, use a head hoop [a thin tube attached to a harness that surrounds the front of the dog's head] to protect your dog from bumping into things and prevent injury," Owens adds. Keep your dog safe by blocking off areas where he could fall — a ditch, pool, stairs or deck. Always walk your dog on a leash or keep him contained in a fenced yard.

SKIN DISEASE

Imagine if your poodle had large, widespread bald patches all over his body and constantly battled skin infections. That was the fear of Gail Fellman of Danville, Calif., when she learned that Chloe, her 4-year-old Standard Poodle, had *sebaceous adenitis*.

"SA is a rare, poorly understood condition in which the sebaceous glands in the skin become inflamed for unknown reasons and are eventually destroyed," says Sandra Sargent, D.V.M., resident in dermatology at the University of Tennessee. "These glands normally produce sebum, a fatty secretion that helps prevent the skin from drying out."

SA is a hereditary disease that occurs in several breeds, including all poodle varieties, but more so in Standards. Owners usually first see signs of SA when their dogs are young adults to middle-aged.

"Clinical signs usually vary significantly between breeds, as well as between

Did You Know?

Across the globe, more than 800 species of ticks exist, and they aren't particular to where they dine. Mammals, birds and reptiles are all fair game.

affected individuals within a breed," Sargent says. "Mild to severe scaling that involves the back, neck, top of head, face and ears is most common. In longer-coated dogs, such as poodles, the scales adhere tightly to the hairs. The coat may be dull, dry, greasy or matted. Patchy to widespread hair loss may be seen. Secondary bacterial infections are common and may cause itching, although SA itself does not typically cause itching. Diagnosis is based on clinical signs and a skin biopsy showing inflammation or complete absence of sebaceous glands."

There is no cure for SA, and management is long term, often with mixed results. "Most important for management is the regular use of anti-seborrheic shampoos to remove the scales and dead hair, together with fatty-acid dietary supplements," Sargent says. "This may be all that's required for mildly affected dogs.

"Additional treatments include spraying the dog with a mixture of propylene glycol and water to help restore lubricants to the skin and using oral essential fatty acids. Because secondary bacterial infections are common, antibiotics may need to be prescribed frequently. Other treatments for more severely affected dogs include oral vitamin A or synthetic retinoids. Recently, cyclosporine, an immuno-suppressant drug, has been effective in some dogs, but is very costly for large-breed dogs."

To manage her dog's condition, Fellman keeps her poodle's coat clipped short. "I apply about one cup of bath oil mixed with a teaspoon of tea tree oil every 10 to 14 days," she says. Sargent says bath oil mixed

SMART TIP!

Brush your dog's teeth every day. Plaque colonizes on the tooth surface in as little as six to eight hours, and if not removed by brushing, forms calculus (tartar) within three to five days. Plaque and tartar cause gum disease, periodontal disease, loosening of the teeth and tooth loss. In bad cases of dental disease, bacteria from the mouth can get into the bloodstream, leading to kidney or heart problems — all of which are life-shortening.

with tree oil is OK, because it's antibacterial and antifungal. However, she cautions, "Tea tree oil can cause drug reactions, so if the skin worsens after application, remove the tea tree oil."

Fellman's next step is to "rinse Chloe off and wash her with an antibacterial, degreasing shampoo. During the winter, I do

this in our bathtub, and Chloe, knowing it's bath time, walks down the hall, goes into the bathroom and gets into the tub — all by herself! I finish her bath with conditioner, leaving most of it on without rinsing. Chloe is really patient, and she lets me do this willingly. Her skin is pretty sensitive on her back and on the top of her head, so I don't brush her excessively." Sometimes, Fellman will just do a quick spot wash on the affected areas.

Recently, Fellman began taking Chloe for acupuncture treatments and switched her diet to a fish and sweet-potato kibble, both of which Fellman believes has dramatically helped Chloe's skin.

Fortunately, Chloe responded well to her therapy. At 10½ years old, Chloe had never developed bald spots or secondary skin infections. "To look at her today, you would never know she has a problem, other than her top knot is thin and straight — a result of her SA," Fellman says.

Although other health disorders are starting to slow her down, such as emphysema and related respiratory problems, Chloe still remains active by doing therapy visits at schools for physically and developmentally disabled children, assisted-living centers for seniors and at an Alzheimer's day-care center. "Chloe is sweet, loving and gentle," Fellman says. "She lets our two granddaughters dress her up in their play clothes. Chloe is definitely a once-in-a-lifetime companion."

it's a **Fact**

In young puppies, roundworms cause bloated bellies, diarrhea and vomiting, and are transmitted from the mother (through blood or milk). Affected pups will not appear as animated as normal puppies. The worms appear spaghetti-like, measuring as long as 6 inches!

Imagining a beautiful poodle with skin problems is difficult, but *sebaceous adenitis* causes just that.

ADDISON'S DISEASE

The crisis came on suddenly. One day, Cosette, a 14-month-old Standard Poodle, was extremely happy and healthy; the next morning, she was unusually quiet and refused her breakfast. "We took her to the vet and they found out she was dehydrated," says owner Mary Ann Eustis of Lynchburg, Va. "Because she had been gnawing on things like sticks, pebbles and horse-hoof parings, they assumed that her GI tract was irritated, rehydrated her with a saline solution and sent her home with some antibiotics."

Although Cosette perked up with the fluid treatment, as the effects wore off, she again lost her appetite and became lethargic. During the next appointment, while Cosette's veterinarian was taking X-rays to see if the young Poodle had some sort of obstruction, Cosette collapsed. She was given a shot of dexamethasone (an anti-inflammatory agent), more fluids and was admitted the next day to a veterinary teaching hospital.

"Her weight had dropped from 43 to 34 pounds in one week, and as I cradled her in my arms, her heartbeat was only about 50 beats per minute," Eustis says. "The prognosis was grim, and they initially diagnosed Cosette with kidney failure, predicting that we might be able to nurse her through another year or so. Then the vet burst into the room with a huge smile on her face. She told us she had reviewed the bloodwork and was pretty sure she knew what the problem was and that Cosette wasn't going to die. It was Addison's disease, and it was treatable."

Addison's disease is a great imitator, says Douglas Brum, D.V.M., staff veterinarian at Angell Animal Medical Center in Boston, Mass. The clinical signs can be vague and varied, with bloodwork often falsely suggesting some other problem.

An inherited disorder, Addison's disease refers to a decreased or complete lack of function of the adrenal glands. "The adrenal glands produce different types of hormones, including glucocorticoids and mineralocorticoids," Brum says. "These are steroid hormones that control many different body functions, such as GI function, mental activity and electrolytes. The adrenal glands also help the body adapt to stressful situations."

The disease is more common in spayed or neutered dogs, is usually diagnosed in dogs between the ages of 2 to 5 years, and is seen more in certain breeds, including poodles.

A dog that is deficient in either or both of these hormones could display extremely subtle changes, Brum says. "Waxing and waning illness, slight GI problems, mild lethargy or signs that only occur when the animal is stressed," he says.

"They feel bad for a day or two, then feel fine," Brum explains. "They have an intermittent GI problem, then they feel fine. Alternatively, the dog can become pretty sick and develop life-threatening problems; the electrolytes can become very abnormal, causing heart problems, and the dog may become dehydrated extremely quickly, possibly going into shock and dying."

Other times with AD, bloodwork, electrolytes and heart function can be normal — or not. Sometimes blood sugar levels can drop, potassium and renal levels become raised, heart rate slows or arrhythmias develop. Any of these abnormalities can be attributed to other various disorders.

Fortunately, there is a way to definitively diagnosis AD through an ACTH stimulation test. "We administer ACTH, a hormone, that stimulates the adrenal glands," Brum says. "We measure a baseline cortisol level, give the ACTH hormone, wait an hour, then take a post-sample. In normal dogs, we should see a significant rise in that cortisol level. If there isn't an appropriate response, the dog has Addison's disease."

Addison's has no cure, but in the majority of cases, it can be successfully managed, with affected dogs living normally. "Dog owners or their vets can inject their dogs about once a month with DOCP, a synthetic hormone," Brum says. "Or, they can give Florinef pills [a mineralocortoid that regulates electrolytes in the body] once or twice a day. Most Addisonian dogs will also need to be on a small dose of prednisone [a glucocorticoid, similar to cortisol]. Some seem to do better on one protocol than on the other; some may drink a lot of water and urinate a lot when on one regimen, or vice versa, so you may need to switch to the other protocol."

Often, the veterinarian will have to adjust the initial dosage to find the correct amount and intervals that work best for the dog. The dog should also be re-tested occasionally because dosage requirements can sometimes change.

After Cosette was diagnosed and put on the appropriate medication, she bounced right back, living an otherwise normal life until dying of unrelated causes at 9 years of age. "There were a few bumps in the road because any minor problem can turn into a major issue if you don't control the Addison's," Eustis says. "We were cautious about getting her to the vet at the first sign of problems. But she was a bouncy Standard Poodle, and nobody would have ever guessed she had a life-threatening illness.

"The vets were right," Eustis continues. "Cosette enjoyed a wonderful life. She traveled with us, she competed in obedience and agility, she ran around the property with the horses. She led a full and happy life."

BOTTOM LINE

Although some poodles experience health problems known in the breed, remember that no species of animal exists in which every individual is perfectly healthy. Humans, purebred dogs, random-bred dogs and all domestic and wild animals have some predisposition, somewhere, toward specific health problems. However, just because a predisposition exists doesn't mean that it will manifest itself in an individual. Chances are, your poodle will live out his days without ever encountering epilepsy, vision loss, SA or AD.

However, should your poodle exhibit changes in its behavior, personality or activities, be sure to seek veterinary help. Obtaining an accurate, prompt diagnosis and initiating appropriate veterinary care can increase both the quality and quantity of your poodle's life.

CHAPTER 8

NUTRITIONAL

You have probably heard it a thousand times: You are what you eat. Believe it or not, it is very true. For poodles, they are what you feed them because they have little choice in the matter. Even smart owners who want to feed their poodles the best often cannot do so because it can be so confusing. With the overwhelming assortment of dog foods, it's difficult to figure out which one is truly best for their dogs.

BASIC TYPES

Dog foods are produced in various types: dry, wet, semimoist and frozen.

Dry food is useful for cost-conscious owners because it tends to be less expensive than the others. These foods also contain the least fat and the most preservatives. Dry food is bulky and takes longer to eat than other foods, so it's more filling.

Wet food — available in cans or foil pouches — is usually 60 to 70 percent water and is more expensive than dry food. A palatable source of concentrated nutrition, wet food also makes a good supplement for underweight dogs or those recovering from illnesses. Some smart owners

it's a Fact Bones can cause gastro-intestinal obstruction and perforation, and may be contaminated with salmonella or E. coli. Leave them in the trash and give your dog a nylon toy bone instead.

add a little wet food to dry food to increase its appeal.

Semimoist food is flavorful, but it usually contains lots of sugar. That can lead to dental problems and obesity. Therefore, semimoist food is not a good choice for your poodle's main diet.

Likewise, **frozen food**, which is available in cooked and in raw forms, is usually more expensive than wet foods. The advantages of frozen food are similar to those of wet foods.

The amount of food that your poodle needs depends on a number of factors, such as his age, activity level, the quality of the food, reproductive status (if your poodle is a female) and size. What's the easiest way to figure it out? Start with the manufacturer's recommended amount, then adjust it according to your dog's response. For example, feed the recommended amount for a few weeks, and if your poodle loses weight, increase the amount by 10 to 20 percent. If your poodle gains weight, decrease the amount. It won't take long to determine the amount of food that keeps your best friend in optimal condition.

NUTRITION 101

All poodles (and all dogs, for that matter) need proteins, carbohydrates, fats, vitamins and minerals to be in peak condition.

■ **Proteins** are used for growth and repair of muscles, bones and other tissues. They're also used for the production of antibodies, enzymes and hormones. All dogs need protein, but it's especially important for puppies because they grow and develop so quickly. Protein sources include various types of meat, meat meal, meat byproducts, eggs, dairy products and soybeans.

■ **Carbohydrates** are metabolized into glucose, the body's principal energy source. Carbohydrates are available as sugars, starches and fiber.

• Sugars (simple carbohydrates) are not suitable nutrient sources for dogs.

• Starches — a preferred carbohydrate in dog food — are found in a variety of plant products. Starches must be cooked in order to be digested.

• Fiber (cellulose) — also a preferred type of carbohydrate found in dog food — isn't digestible, but helps the digestive tract function properly.

■ **Fats** are also a source of energy and play an important role in maintaining your poodle's skin and coat health, hormone production, nervous system function and vitamin transport. However, you must be aware that fats increase the palatability and

Your poodle can't read the labels, so he looks to you to provide the best possible nutrition that you can afford.

Believe it or not, during your poodle's lifetime, you'll buy a few thousand pounds of dog food! Go to **DogChannel.com/Club-Poodle** and download a chart that outlines the cost of dog food.

Because semimoist food contains lots of sugar, it isn't a good selection for your poodle's main menu. However, it is great for an occasional yummy snack. Try forming into little meatballs for a once-a-week treat! She'll love ya for it!

the calorie count of dog food, which can lead to serious health problems, such as obesity, for puppies or dogs who are allowed to overindulge. Some foods contain added amounts of omega fatty acids such as docosohexaenoic acid, a compound that may enhance brain development and learning in puppies but is not considered an essential nutrient by the Association of American Feed Control Officials (www. aafco.org). Fats used in dog foods include tallow, lard, poultry fat, fish oil and vegetable oils.

■ **Vitamins** and **minerals** are essential to dogs for proper muscle and nerve function, bone growth, healing, metabolism and fluid balance. Especially important for your poodle puppy are calcium, phosphorus and vitamin D, which must be supplied in the right balance to ensure proper development and maintenance of bones and teeth.

Just as your dog receives proper nutrition from his food, water is essential, as well. It keeps your dog's body hydrated and facilitates normal function of the body's systems. During housetraining, it is necessary to keep an eye on how much water your poodle is drinking, but once he is reliably trained, he should have access to clean, fresh water at all times, especially if you feed him dry food. Make sure that your dog's water bowl is clean, and change the water often.

CHECK OUT THE LABEL

To help you get a feel for what you are feeding your dog, start by taking a look at the label on the package or can. Look for the words "complete and balanced." This tells you that the food meets specific nutritional requirements set by the AAFCO for either adults ("maintenance") or puppies and pregnant/lactating females ("growth and reproduction"). The label must state the group for which the food is intended. If you're feeding a puppy, choose a "growth and reproduction" food.

The nutrition label also includes a list of minimum protein, minimum fat, maximum fiber and maximum moisture content. (You won't find carbohydrate content because it's everything that isn't protein, fat, fiber and moisture.)

The nutritional analysis refers to crude protein and crude fat — amounts that have been determined in the laboratory. This analysis is technically accurate, but it does not tell you anything about digestibility: how much of the particular nutrient your poodle can actually use. For information about digestibility, contact the manufacturer (check the label for a telephone number and website address).

Virtually all commercial puppy foods exceed the AAFCO's minimum requirements for protein and fat, the two nutrients most commonly evaluated when comparing foods. Protein levels in dry puppy foods usually range from about 26 to 30 percent; for canned foods, the values are about 9 to 13 percent. The fat content of dry puppy foods is about 20 percent or more; for canned foods, it's 8 percent or more. (Dry food values are larger than canned food values because dry

Dogs of all ages love treats and table food, but these goodies can unbalance your poodle's diet and lead to a weight problem if you don't feed him wisely. Table food, whether fed as a treat or as part of a meal, shouldn't account for more than 10 percent of your dog's daily caloric intake. If you plan to give your poodle treats, be sure to include "treat calories" when calculating her daily food requirement — so you don't end up with a pudgy pup!

When shopping for packaged treats, look for ones that provide complete nutrition. They're basically dog food in a fun form. Choose crunchy goodies for chewing fun and dental health. Other ideas for tasty treats include:

- ✓ small chunks of cooked, lean meat
- ✓ dry dog food morsels
- ✓ cheese
- ✓ veggies (cooked, raw or frozen)
- ✓ breads, crackers or dry cereal
- ✓ unsalted, unbuttered, plain, popped popcorn

Some foods, however, can be dangerous or even deadly to a dog. The following can cause digestive upset (vomiting or diarrhea) or fatal toxic reactions:

- ✗ **avocados:** if eaten in sufficient quantity these can cause gastrointestinal irritation, with vomiting and diarrhea
- ✗ **baby food:** may contain onion powder; does not provide balanced nutrition
- ✗ **chocolate:** contains methylxanthines and theobromine, caffeine-like compounds that can cause vomiting, diarrhea, heart abnormalities, tremors, seizures and death. Darker chocolates contain higher levels of the toxic compounds.
- ✗ **eggs, raw:** Whites contain an enzyme that prevents uptake of biotin, a B vitamin; may contain salmonella.
- ✗ **garlic (and related foods):** can cause gastrointestinal irritation and anemia if eaten in sufficient quantity
- ✗ **grapes:** can cause kidney failure if eaten in sufficient quantity (the toxic dose varies from dog to dog)
- ✗ **macadamia nuts:** can cause vomiting, weakness, lack of coordination and other problems
- ✗ **meat, raw:** may contain harmful bacteria such as salmonella or E. coli
- ✗ **milk:** can cause diarrhea in some puppies
- ✗ **onions (and related foods):** can cause gastrointestinal irritation and anemia if eaten in sufficient quantity
- ✗ **raisins:** can cause kidney failure if eaten in sufficient quantity (the toxic dose varies from dog to dog)
- ✗ **yeast bread dough:** can rise in the gastrointestinal tract, causing obstruction; produces alcohol as it rises

food contains less water; the values are similar when compared on a dry matter basis.)

Finally, check the ingredients on the label, which lists the ingredients in descending order by weight. Manufacturers are allowed to list separately different forms of a single ingredient (e.g., ground corn and corn gluten meal). The food may contain meat byproducts, meat and bone meal, and animal fat, which probably won't appeal to you but are nutritious and safe for your puppy. Higher quality foods usually have meat or meat products near the top of the ingredient list, but you don't need to worry about grain products as long as the label indicates that the food is nutritionally complete. Dogs are omnivores (not carnivores, as commonly believed), so all balanced dog foods contain animal and plant ingredients.

STORE IT RIGHT

Properly storing your poodle's food will ensure that it maintains its quality, nutrient content and taste. Here's what to do before and after you open that package or can.

◆ Dry food should be stored in a cool, dry, bug- and vermin-free place, especially if it's a preservative-free product. Many manufacturers include an expiration date on the package label, but this usually refers to the shelf life of the unopened package. For optimal quality, don't buy more dry food than your poodle can eat in one month. To store dry food after opening the bag, fold the bag top down several times and secure it with a clip or empty the contents into a food-grade airtight plastic container (available at pet-supply stores and discount stores). Make sure the storage container is clean and dry and has never been used to store toxic materials.

◆ Canned food, if unopened, can remain good for three years or longer, but it's best to use it within one year of purchase. Discard puffy cans or those that are leaking fluid. Leftover canned food should be covered and refrigerated, then used within three days.

◆ Frozen food can be stored for at least one year in the freezer. Longer storage can cause deterioration of the quality and taste of the food. Thaw frozen food in the refrigerator or use the defrost setting of your microwave. Cover and refrigerate leftovers, which should be used within 24 hours.

STAGES OF LIFE

When selecting your dog's diet, three stages of development must be considered: the puppy stage, the adult stage and the senior stage.

Feeding your poodle is part of your daily routine. Take a break, and have some fun online by playing "Feed the Poodle." It's fun, it's free and it can only be found at **DogChannel.com/Club-Poodle** — just click on "Games."

SMART TIP!

How can you tell if your poodle is fit or fat?
When you run your hands down your pal's sides from front to back, you should be able to easily feel her ribs. It's OK if you feel a little body fat (and a lot of hair), but you shouldn't feel huge fat pads. You should also be able to feel your poodle's waist — an indentation behind the ribs.

Puppy Diets: Pups instinctively want to nurse, and a normal puppy will exhibit this behavior from just a few moments following birth. Puppies should be allowed to nurse for about the first six weeks, although by the third or fourth week, the breeder will begin to introduce small portions of suitable solid food. Most breeders like to initially introduce alternate milk and solid food meals, leading up to weaning time.

By the time poodle puppies are 7 weeks old (or a maximum of 8), they should be fully weaned and fed solely on puppy food. Selection of the most suitable, high-quality food at this time is essential because a puppy's fastest growth rate is during the first year of life. Seek advice about your dog's diet from your veterinarian. The frequency of meals will be reduced over time, and when a young dog has reached 10 to 12 months, he should be switched to an adult diet.

Puppy and junior diets can be well balanced for the needs of your poodle so that, except in certain circumstances, additional vitamin, mineral and protein supplements will not be required.

How often should you feed your poodle in a day? Puppies have small stomachs and high metabolic rates, so they need to eat several times a day to consume sufficient nutri-ents. If your puppy is younger than 3 months old, feed him four or five meals a day. When your poodle is 3 to 5 months old, decrease the number of meals to three or four. At 6 months, most puppies can move to an adult schedule of two meals a day.

Adult Diets: A dog is considered an adult when he has stopped growing. Rely on your veterinarian or dietary specialist to recommend an acceptable maintenance diet. Major dog food manufacturers specialize in this type of food, and smart owners must select the one best suited to their dogs' needs. Do not leave food out all day for free feeding, as this freedom inevitably translates to inches around the dog's waist.

Senior Diets: As dogs get older, their metabolism begins to change. A senior poodle usually exercises less, moves more slowly and sleeps more.

This change in his lifestyle and physiological performance requires a change in diet. Because these changes take place slowly, they might not be recognizable at first. These metabolic changes increase the tendency toward obesity, requiring an even more vigilant approach to feeding. Obesity in an older dog exacerbates the health problems that already accompany old age.

As a poodle ages, few of his organs will function up to par. The kidneys slow down, and the intestines become less efficient. These age-related factors are best handled with a change in diet and a change in feeding schedule to give smaller portions that are more easily digested.

There is no single best diet for an older poodle. While many older dogs will do perfectly fine on light or senior diets, other dogs will do better on special premium diets such as lamb and rice. Be sensitive to your senior poodle's diet, and this will help control other problems that may arise with your old friend.

A healthy coat begins
with a proper diet.

A healthy dog needs access to plenty of fresh, clean water all day long.

These delicious, dog-friendly recipes will have your furry friend smacking her lips and salivating for more. Just remember: Treats aren't meant to replace your dog's regular meals. Give your poodle snacks sparingly and continue to feed her nutritious, well-balanced meals.

Cheddar Squares

$1/3$ cup all-natural applesauce
$1/3$ cup low-fat cheddar cheese, shredded
$1/3$ cup water
2 cups unbleached white flour

In a medium bowl, mix all the wet ingredients. In a large bowl, mix all the dry ingredients. Slowly add all the wet ingredients to the dry mixture.

Mix well. Pour batter into a greased, 13x9x2-inch pan. Bake at 375-degrees Fahrenheit for 25 to 30 minutes. Bars are done when a toothpick inserted in the center and removed comes out clean. Cool and cut into bars. This recipe makes about 54, $1^1/_2$-inch bars.

Peanut Butter Bites

3 tablespoons vegetable oil
$1/4$ cup smooth peanut butter, no salt or sugar
$1/4$ cup honey
$1^1/_2$ teaspoon baking powder
2 eggs
2 cups whole wheat flour

In a large bowl, mix all ingredients until dough is firm. If the dough is too sticky, mix in a small amount of flour. Knead dough on a lightly floured surface until firm. Roll out dough half an inch thick, and cut with cookie cutters. Put cookies on a cookie sheet half an inch apart. Bake at 350-degrees Fahrenheit for 20 to 25 minutes. When done, cookies should be firm to the touch. Turn oven off and leave cookies for one to two hours to harden. This recipe makes about 40, 2-inch-long cookies.

YOUR POODLE

The elegant and graceful poodle is truly an aristocratic-looking dog. Originally a water retriever of great repute, today's poodle is loved and spoiled worldwide as a beloved family pet. Part of what gives the poodle his stylish reputation is his beautiful, long coat, which can be clipped and shaped in a variety of ways.

The most elaborate coat clips can be seen in the show ring, where pompons and bracelets are carefully clipped and hand-scissored to perfection by professional handlers and groomers. Although every poodle is a winner in the eyes of his owner, most don't need to wear a long, glamorous show clip while sitting around on the couch at home. With a little attention and consistency, anyone can learn how to easily groom a poodle.

Grooming is an essential part of keeping your poodle healthy, happy and looking good. It's important to plan on establishing a consistent grooming routine when you add a puppy to your family, or to start one with an older dog. Coat care is a large part of grooming your poodle, but taking care of his teeth, nails and ears should also be part of your dog's grooming regime.

Did You Know? **Nail clipping can be tricky, so many dog owners leave the task for the professionals.** However, if you walk your dog on concrete, you may not have to worry about it. The concrete acts like a nail file and will help keep the nails neatly trimmed.

UNDERSTANDING
THE POODLE COAT

The poodle coat is composed of individual hairs that grow continuously; meaning they can continue growing longer, rather than reaching a certain length and stopping. The poodle coat grabs onto dead hair, which is why the breed is considered an excellent choice for anyone allergic to dogs. Because of this, it's extremely important that these dogs are brushed on a regular basis to remove dead hair. If not removed manually

through brushing and bathing, the dead hair becomes severely matted.

As puppies, some poodles go through what is referred to as a coat change, which can last about one month for Toy Poodles and two to three months for Standards. A poodle puppy has a soft coat, which usually falls in gentle waves or soft curls. At approximately 9 to 16 months of age, the coat undergoes a change in texture, becoming thicker and coarser. During this period, the coat tends to mat easily and requires extra attention and brushing.

TO GROOM OR NOT TO GROOM

You need to decide whether you want to learn how to care for and clip your poodle's coat yourself or whether you'll visit a professional groomer every four to six weeks. Even if you decide to use a professional groomer, you'll still need to do some weekly coat care. "Poodle owners can absolutely learn how to clip and shape their dog's coat," says Chris Manelotoulos, a professional poodle handler from Greensboro, N.C. "It's not difficult to learn, but it does involve an investment in some basic equipment and time,"

Although it's not difficult to learn, clipping your dog's coat does require someone to show you the basics. You can buy videos and books that explain how to clip a poodle's coat, but nothing compares to having someone show you in person. "If you want to learn how to keep your poodle in a short pet clip, the breeder you buy your puppy from should be willing to show you how it's done," says Penny Dugan, a poodle breeder from Bothell, Wash.

Manelotoulos agrees. "You don't just want to buy a pair of clippers and see what happens," he says. "You need to learn the basics, including how to properly hold and

NOTABLE & QUOTABLE

After removing a tick, clean your dog's skin with hydrogen peroxide. If Lyme disease is common where you live, have your veterinarian test the tick. Tick preventive medication will discourage ticks from attaching and kill any that do.

— groomer Andrea Vilardi from West Paterson, N.J.

use scissors and clippers." If you do decide to take on the task of maintaining your poodle's clip, you need to invest in the right equipment, which usually includes a slicker brush, metal combs, a mat rake, scissors, electric clippers with three to four different blade sizes and a good dryer, preferably a stand-alone one.

However, in today's fast-paced world, you might decide to use a groomer to keep your poodle's coat clipped. In this case, a professional groomer does a thorough grooming, including bathing, drying, clipping and shaping your poodle's coat. A shorter coat is much easier to maintain.

THE FASHIONABLE POODLE TRIM

The poodle is considered the national dog of France. Of course, who else but the French would claim such a stylish breed with a variety of fashionable clips as their own? Big or small, a poodle's coat creates a statement.

No one knows for certain where the poodle's chic clips began. Some believe that huntsmen trimmed the poodle in order to improve the dog's ability to swim through water, avoid snagging on underbrush and keep his joints and organs warm and protected from the cold. Others believe that the poodle's specialized clips came from their early days as performance dogs with the cir-

cus. Whatever the case, here is a brief overview of common poodle clips. In the American Kennel Club show ring, all poodles older than 12 months must be shown in either the Continental or English Saddle clip.

Puppy Show: This clip can be seen in the show ring on poodles younger than 12 months of age. The coat is long but the face, throat, feet and base of the tail are shaved. The shaven feet are visible, and there is a pompon on the end of the tail. The pet puppy cut is slightly shorter.

English Saddle: The face, throat, feet, forelegs and base of the tail are shaved. A puff is left on each foreleg and a pompon on the end of the tail. The hindquarters are covered with a short blanket of hair except for a curved, shaved area on each flank and two shaved bands on each hindleg. The shaven feet and a portion of the shaven leg above the puff are visible. The rest of the body is left in full coat but may be shaped in order to ensure overall balance.

Continental: The face, throat, feet and base of the tail are shaved. The hindquarters are shaved with optional pompons on the hips. The legs are shaved, leaving a bracelet on each hindleg and a puff on each foreleg. There is a pompon on the end of the tail. The shaven feet and a portion of the shaven foreleg above the puff are visible. The rest of the body is left in full coat but may be shaped in order to ensure overall balance.

Sporting or Kennel: The face, feet, throat and base of tail are shaved, leaving a scissored cap on the top of the head and a pompon on the end of the tail. The rest of the body and legs are clipped or scissored to follow the outline of the dog, leaving a short blanket of coat no longer than 1 inch in length. The hair on the legs may be slightly longer than that on the body.

Socialize your puppy to grooming sessions, so he'll be ready when he needs a bath as an adult.

Dutch: The head and ears are clipped to one-quarter inch, leaving only a fringe at the bottom. The topknot is rounded off. The chest, stomach and back of the dog are clipped to one-quarter inch, leaving the long hair on all four legs either squared off above the shoulders or coming to a point higher up. Feet and tail are clipped.

Corded: It's unusual to see a poodle with a corded coat, but they do exist. The coat is allowed to grow extremely long and the hair cords together, creating a long rope-like appearance. Any poodle with a correct coat can be corded once his adult coat has come in. The coat will start to cord between 9 and 18 months. Establishing the cords is a lot of work, but they're fairly easy to maintain once they have some length. Cords cannot be brushed out and have to be clipped off.

COAT MAINTENANCE

Between clippings, a poodle's coat needs at least a weekly brushing. "For a weekly brushing, I use a slicker brush and a fine-tooth comb," Dugan says. "I brush the coat out first to break up any mats, then I comb through it." The comb will help you find any tangles or mats you may have missed. Start with a small, manageable section of hair. Insert the teeth of the slicker brush at the bottom of the hair (avoid the skin) and pull up with the brush. This makes the coat fluffy.

Debbi Foust, a professional groomer from Graham, Wash., says, "It's important to brush in a straight line, all the way down to a poo-dle's skin because mats start at the skin." Foust also suggests starting to brush your poodle at the nose and working your way toward the rear. Every part of a poodle's coat, including the legs and underside, retains dead hair, so brush it thoroughly.

"When people get a puppy, I suggest they get the pup accustomed to being touched in all kinds of positions — for instance sitting, standing and lying on his back," Foust says. "It's much easier to groom the underside of a poodle, especially the armpits, where a lot of matting occurs, if the dog will lie on his back." This weekly brushing routine should keep your poodle's coat in good condition and mat-free.

In addition to brushing the coat on a weekly basis, Foust suggests conditioning it to help prevent hair breakage. "Fill a spray bottle with water mixed with a small amount of dog-safe conditioner and lightly mist the coat before brushing," she says. If your poodle gets extra dirty and needs a bath between professional groomings, make sure to use a shampoo and conditioner specifically formulated for dogs. These products are made for a dog's coat and are usually nonirritating if they accidentally get in their eyes.

POODLE PEDICURES

Keeping a poodle's nails trimmed is an important part of the grooming routine. "poodles have beautiful feet and walk up on their toes," Dugan says. "If their nails get too long, they won't be able to walk properly."

When your poodle gets dirty or muddy, you'll need to give him a bath between regular grooming visits.

A professional groomer will trim your dog's nails during the grooming session, but because these visits occur every four to six weeks, you'll also need to trim your dog's nails at home, preferably weekly, to keep them short.

To trim your dog's nails at home you'll need nail clippers and styptic powder or pencil (a blood coagulant). You can purchase either scissor- or guillotine-type nail-clippers. Each type works equally well, but most people find they have a definite preference for one or the other.

In the center of each toenail is the blood and nerve supply for the nail, called the "quick." With light nails, you can identify the quick by its pink color. For dark nails, you can shine a flashlight behind the nail to locate the quick. Trim the tips of the nails as close to the quick as possible without cutting into it because it will bleed and cause your dog pain. If you accidentally cut into the quick and bleeding occurs, apply a dab of styptic powder to the nail with gentle pressure until it stops bleeding.

Another option for keeping your poodle's nails short is an electric nail grinder, which uses a rotating sandpaper bit to shorten the nails. Some dogs prefer the grinder to clippers. "If you start out with short nails, all you need to do is use a grinder once a week for a few seconds on each nail," Manelotoulos says.

it's a Fact

Dogs can't rinse and spit after a brushing, so doggie toothpaste must be safe for pets to swallow. Always use a toothpaste specially formulated for dogs when brushing your poodle's teeth.

One drawback to the electric grinder is that any hair around your dog's nails can get caught in it. "A good trick for keeping hair away from the grinder is to put an old nylon stocking over your dog's foot and poke the nails through the nylon," Foust says. "This keeps any hair on the feet away from the grinder."

Whatever method you decide to use, nail trimming sessions need to be part of your weekly grooming routine to keep your poodle's feet in good shape. If you start nail trimmings when your poodle is a puppy, you'll find he'll be much more amenable to the process when he's grown.

EAR AND TEETH CARE

Clean your poodle's ears about once a week with a cleaning solution (available at pet-supply stores) made for dog's ears. You can easily do this at home as needed when your poodle's ears are dirty (when you see dark-colored debris in his ear).

Simply squirt the cleaning solution inside the ear canal, according to the product's directions, then massage the outside of the ear at its base

for approximately 30 seconds. Use a cotton ball to clean any loose debris and excess fluid from the ear leather and as much of the ear canal as you can easily access with the cotton ball. Don't dig too deeply into the ear canal with cotton balls or swabs because you might damage the inner ear. Repeat this procedure until there's no more debris.

Because dogs tend to smile with their waggy tails instead of with their mouths, it's easy to forget about dental care. However, dental care is an extremely

A poodle shouldn't be caught in the middle of a power struggle between children and parents.
Divvy up grooming and bathing responsibilities early on, and make the issue non-negotiable. A clean poodle is welcomed into the house; a dirty one is banished to the backyard, always on the outside looking in.

important part of your poodle's grooming routine. Eighty-five percent of all dogs have some type of dental disease by the age of 3, so it's important to learn to brush your poodle's teeth to prevent the build up of plaque and keep those teeth healthy. Brush your dog's teeth as often as possible; every day is best, but do it as often as you can.

All you need is two basic pieces of equipment: toothpaste and a toothbrush. Make sure to use toothpaste formulated for dogs, which comes in yummy flavors, such as chicken and beef. Don't use human toothpaste on your poodle because it's not meant to be swallowed and can irritate your dog's stomach.

Next, you'll need a toothbrush. Choose one that easily fits in your poodle's mouth. A Toy Poodle is going to need a smaller tooth-brush than a Standard. Purchase these dental supplies at your local pet-supply store or from your veterinarian. If you're looking for small toothbrush, you might try a human pediatric or fingertip one. Other dental-care products are available that can be used to clean teeth, including dental wipes. These wipes come pre-moistened with a plaque inhibitor, and as the name suggests, you wipe them over your dog's teeth.

Ideally, you'll want to start dental care when your poodle is a puppy so he views brushings as a regular part of his grooming routine. Introduce teeth cleaning slowly and gently. Start by letting your poodle lick the toothpaste off your fingers, then sliding your finger with the toothpaste into his mouth. Slowly work up to using the tooth-brush or dental wipes throughout his mouth. Use a circular motion, and just brush the front of the teeth.

In addition to brushing at home, your poodle will need regular professional cleanings performed by a veterinarian. Check with your veterinarian to find out how often your poodle's teeth need a professional cleaning and at what age to start them.

REWARD A JOB WELL DONE

There's nothing more important than the health of your poodle. One of the best ways to monitor your dog's well being is to spend time every week grooming him. Make grooming a special time for you and your dog. This time together gives you an opportunity to notice any changes in your poodle's health as he goes from being a puppy to an adult to a senior. It's easy; all it takes is a little time, some know-how and a lot of love.

Be sure to reward your poodle for behaving well during grooming. This is the best

way to ensure stress-free grooming throughout his lifetime. Bathing energizes your pet, and using the time immediately after grooming as play time is the best way to reward your poodle for a job well done. Watching your clean, healthy poodle tear from room to room in sheer joy is your reward for being a caring owner.

Six Tips for Poodle Care

1. Grooming tools can be scary to some dogs, so let yours see and sniff everything at the start. Keep your beauty sessions short, too. Most poodles don't enjoy standing still for too long.
2. Look at your dog's eyes for any discharge, and her ears for inflammation, debris or foul odor. If you notice anything that doesn't look right, immediately contact your veterinarian.
3. Choose a time to groom your dog when you don't have to rush, and assemble all of the grooming tools before you begin. This way you can focus on your dog's needs instead of having to stop in the middle of the session to search for an item.
4. Start establishing a grooming routine the day after you bring her home. A regular grooming schedule will make it easier to remember what touch-ups your dog needs.
5. Proper nail care helps with your dog's gait and spinal alignment. Nails that are too long can force a dog to walk improperly. Also, too-long nails can snag and tear, causing painful injury to your poodle.
6. Good dental health prevents gum disease and early tooth loss. Brush your poodle's teeth daily and see a veterinarian yearly.

Six Questions to Ask a Groomer

1. Do you cage dry? Are you willing to hand dry or air dry my pet?
2. What type of shampoo are you using? Is it tearless? If not, do you have a tearless variety available for use?
3. Will you restrain my pet if she acts up during nail clipping? What methods do you use to handle difficult dogs?
4. Are you familiar with the poodle? Do you have any references from other poodle owners?
5. Is the shop air-conditioned during hot weather?
6. Will my dog be getting brushed or just bathed?

TIME TO

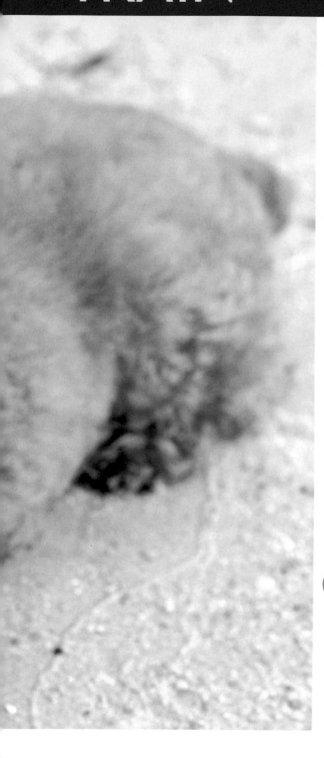

Reward-based training methods — clicking and luring — instruct dogs on what to do and help them do it correctly, setting them up for success and rewards rather than mistakes and punishment.

CLICK THIS!

A clicker is a small, plastic device that makes a sharp clicking sound when a button is pressed. You can purchase them at any pet-supply store. It is used in a training method that precisely marks a desired behavior so your dog knows exactly which behavior earned a reward.

When using a clicker, you "charge" the clicker by clicking and giving your poodle a treat several times, until he understands that the click means he gets a treat. The click then becomes a secondary reinforcer. It's not the reward itself, but it will become so closely linked with a reward in your dog's mind that it has the same effect as a reward.

Next, you click the clicker when your poodle does any desirable behavior. Then, you follow it up with a click and treat. The click exactly marks, more pre-

Did You Know? **The prime period for socialization is short.** Most behavior experts agree that positive experiences during the period between 4 and 14 weeks of age are vital to the development of a puppy who'll grow into an adult dog with sound temperament.

cisely than a word or gesture, the desired behavior, quickly teaching your poodle which behaviors will earn rewards.

Most dogs find food rewards meaningful; poodles are no exception as they tend to be food-motivated. This works well because positive training relies on using treats, at least initially, to encourage a dog to demonstrate a certain behavior. The treat is then given as a reward. When you reinforce desired behaviors with rewards that are valuable to your dog, you are met with happy cooperation rather than resistance.

Positive reinforcement does not necessarily equal passivity. While you are rewarding your poodle's desirable behaviors, you must still manage him to be sure he isn't getting rewarded for his undesirable behaviors. Training tools, such as leashes, tethers, gates and crates, help keep your dog out of trouble. The use of force-free negative punishment (the dog's behavior makes a good thing go away) helps him realize there are negative consequences for inappropriate behaviors.

LEARNING SOCIAL GRACES

Now that you have done all of the preparatory work and have helped your poodle get accustomed to his new home and family, it's time for you to have some fun! Socializing your puppy gives you the opportunity to show off your new friend, and your poodle gets to reap the benefits of being an adorable little creature whom people will want to pet and gush over how precious he is.

Besides getting to know his new family, your puppy should be exposed to other people, animals and situations; but, of course, he must not come into close contact with dogs who you don't know well until he has had all his vaccinations. This will help him become well adjusted as he grows up and less prone to being timid or fearful of the new things he will encounter.

Your pup's socialization began at the breeder's home, but now it is your responsibility to continue it. The socialization he receives up until he is 12 weeks of age is the most critical, as this is the time when he forms his impressions of the outside world. Be especially careful during the 8- to 10-week period, also known as the fear period. The interaction he receives during this time should be gentle and reassuring. Lack of socialization can manifest itself in fear and aggression as your poodle matures. Puppies require a lot of human contact, affection, handling and exposure to other animals.

Once your poodle has received his necessary vaccinations, feel free to take him out and about (on his leash, of course). Walk him around the neighborhood, take him on your daily errands, let people pet him and let him meet other dogs and pets. Make sure to expose your poodle to different people — men, women, kids, babies, men with beards, teenagers with cell phones or riding skateboards, joggers, shoppers, someone in a wheelchair, a pregnant woman, etc.

SMART TIP!

If your poodle refuses to sit with both haunches squarely beneath her and instead sits on one side or the other, she may have a physical reason for doing so. Discuss the habit with your veterinarian to be certain your dog isn't suffering from some structural problem.

Make sure your poodle explores different surfaces like sidewalks, gravel and even a puddle. Positive experience is the key to building confidence. It's up to you to make sure your poodle safely discovers the world so he will be a calm, confident and well-socialized dog.

It's important that you take the lead in all socialization experiences and never put your pup in a scary or potentially harmful situation. Be mindful of your poodle's limitations. Fifteen minutes at a public market is fine; two hours at a loud outdoor concert is too much. Meeting vaccinated, tolerant and gentle older dogs is great. Meeting dogs who you don't know or trust isn't a great idea, especially if they appear very energetic, dominant or fearful. Control the situations in which you place your puppy.

The best way to socialize your puppy to a new experience is to make him think it's the best thing ever. You can do this with a lot of happy talk, enthusiasm and, yes, food. To convince your puppy that almost any experience is a blast, always carry treats. Consider carrying two types — a bag of his puppy chow, which you can give him when introducing him to nonthreatening experiences, and a bag of high-value, mouth-watering treats to give him when introducing him to unfamiliar experiences.

Training works best when incorporated into daily life. When your poodle asks for something — food, play or whatever else — cue her to do something for you first. Reward her by granting her request.

Practice in different settings, so your poodle learns to listen regardless of her surroundings.

BASIC CUES

All poodles, regardless of your training and relationship goals, need to know at least five basic good-manner behaviors: sit, down, stay, come and heel. Here are tips for teaching your poodle these important cues.

SIT: Every dog should learn to sit.

● Hold a treat at the end of your poodle's nose.

● Move the treat over his head.

● When your dog sits, click a clicker or say "Yes!"

● Feed your dog the treat.

● If your dog jumps up, hold the treat lower. If he backs up, back him into a corner and wait until he sits. Be patient. Keep your clicker handy, and click (or say "Yes!") and treat anytime he offers a sit.

● When he is able to easily offers sits, say "sit" just before he offers, so he can make the association between the word and the behavior. Add the sit cue when you know you can get the behavior. Your dog doesn't know what the word means until you repeatedly associate it with the appropriate behavior.

● When your poodle sits easily on cue, start using intermittent reinforcement by clicking some sits but not others. At first, click most sits and skip an occasional one (this is a high rate of reinforcement). Gradually make your clicks random.

DOWN: If your poodle can sit, then he can learn to lie down.

◆ Have your poodle sit.

◆ Hold the treat in front of his nose. Move it down slowly, straight toward the floor (toward his toes). If he follows all the way down, click and treat.

◆ If he gets stuck, move the treat down slowly. Click and treat for small movements downward — moving his head a bit lower, or inching one paw forward. Keep clicking and treating until your poodle is all the way down. This training method is called "shaping" — rewarding small pieces of a behavior until your dog succeeds.

◆ If your dog stands as you move the treat toward the floor, have him sit, and move the treat even more slowly downward, shaping with clicks and treats for small, downward movements. If he stands, cheerfully say "Oops!" (which means "Sorry, no treat for that!"), have him sit and try again.

◆ If shaping isn't working, sit on the floor with your knee raised. Have your poodle sit next to you. Put your hand with the treat under your knee and lure him under your leg so he lies down and crawls to follow the treat. Click and treat!

◆ When you can lure the down easily, add the verbal cue, wait a few seconds to let your dog think, then lure him down to show him the association. Repeat until your poodle goes down on the verbal cue; then begin using intermittent reinforcement.

STAY: What good are sit and down cues if your dog doesn't stay?

▲ Start with your poodle in a sit or down position.

With the proper training, your poodle will be as well behaved as she is adorable. One certification that all dogs should receive is the American Kennel Club Canine Good Citizen, which rewards dogs with good manners. Go to **DogChannel.com/Club-Poodle** and click on "Downloads" to get the 10 steps required for your dog to be a CGC.

▲ Put the treat in front of your dog's nose and keep it there.

▲ Click and reward several times while he is in position, then release him with a cue you will always use to tell him the stay is over. Common release cues are: "all done," "break," "free," "free dog," "at ease" and "OK."

▲ When your poodle will stay in a sit or down position while you click and treat, add your verbal stay cue. Say "stay," pause for a second or two, click and say "stay" again. Release.

▲ When your poodle is getting the idea, say "stay," whisk the treat out of sight behind your back, click the clicker and whisk the treat back. Be sure to get it all the way to his nose, so he doesn't jump up. Gradually increase the duration of the stay.

▲ When he will stay for 15 to 20 seconds, add small distractions: shuffling your feet, moving your arms, small hops. Gradually increase distractions. If your poodle makes mistakes, it means you're adding too much, too fast.

▲ When he'll stay for 15 to 20 seconds with distractions, gradually add distance. Have your poodle stay, take a half-step back, click, return and treat. When he'll stay with a half-step, tell him to stay, take a full step back, click and return. Always return to your dog to treat after you click, but before you release. If you always return, his stay becomes strong. If you call him to you, his stay gets weaker due to his eagerness to come to you.

COME: A reliable recall — coming when called — can be a challenging behavior to teach. It is possible, however. To succeed, you need to install an automatic response to your "come" cue — one so automatic that your poodle doesn't even stop to think when he hears it, but will spin on his heels and charge to you at full speed.

■ Start by charging a come cue the same way you charged your clicker. If your poodle already ignores the word "come," pick a different cue, like "front" or "hugs." Say your cue and feed him a bit of scrumptious treat. Repeat this until his eyes light up when he hears the cue. Now you're ready to start training.

■ With your poodle on a leash, run away several steps and cheerfully call out your charged cue. When he follows, click the clicker. Feed him a treat when he reaches you. For a more enthusiastic come, run away at full speed as you call him. When he follows at a gallop, stop running, click and give him a treat. The better your poodle gets at coming, the farther away he can be when you call him.

■ Once your poodle understands the come cue, have more people join the exercise, each holding a clicker and treats. Stand a short distance apart and take turns calling and running away. Click and treat in turn as he comes to each of you. Gradually increase the distance until he comes flying to each person from a distance.

it's a
Fact

Behaviors are best trained by breaking them down into their simplest components, teaching those, and then linking them together to end up with the complete behavior. Keep treats small so you can reward many times without stuffing your poodle. Remember, don't bore your poodle; avoid excessive repetition.

When you and your poodle are ready to practice in wide-open spaces, attach a long line — a 20- to 50-foot leash — to your dog, so you can get a hold of him if that taunting squirrel nearby is too much of a temptation. Then, head to a practice area where there are less tempting distractions.

HEEL: Heeling means that your dog can calmly walk beside you without pulling. It takes time and patience on your part to succeed at teaching your dog that you will not proceed unless he is walking beside you with ease. Pulling out ahead on the leash is definitely unacceptable.

● Begin by holding the leash in your left hand as your poodle sits beside your left leg. Move the loop end of the leash to your right hand but keep your left hand short on the leash so it keeps your dog close to you.

● Say "heel" and step forward on your left foot. Keep your poodle close to you and take three steps. Stop and have your dog sit next to you in what we now call the heel position. Praise verbally, but do not touch your dog. Hesitate a moment and begin again with "heel," taking three steps and stopping, at which point your dog is told to sit again.

Your goal here is to have your dog walk those three steps without pulling on the leash. Once he will walk calmly beside you for three steps without pulling, increase the number of steps you take to five. When he will walk politely beside you while you take five steps, you can increase the length of your walk to 10 steps. Keep increasing the length of your stroll until your dog will walk beside you without pulling for as long as you want him to heel. When you stop heeling, indicate to your dog that the exer-

SMART TIP!

If you begin teaching the heel cue by taking long walks and letting your dog pull you along, she may misinterpret this action as acceptable. When you pull back on the leash to counteract her pulling, she will read that tug as a signal to pull even harder!

cise is over by petting him and saying "OK, good dog." The "OK" is used as a release word, meaning that the exercise is finished, and he is free to relax.

● If you are dealing with a poodle who insists on pulling you around, simply put on your brakes and stand your ground until

your poodle realizes that the two of you are not going anywhere until he is beside you and moving at your pace, not his. It may take some time just standing there to convince your dog that you are the leader, and you will be the one to decide on the direction and speed of your travel.

● Each time your dog looks up at you or slows down to give a slack leash between the two of you, quietly praise him and say, "Good heel. Good dog." Eventually, your dog will begin to respond, and within a few days he will be walking politely beside you without pulling on the leash. At first, the training sessions should be kept short and very positive; soon your poodle will be able to walk nicely with you for increasingly longer distances. Remember to give your poodle free time and the opportunity to run and play when you have finished heel practice.

TRAINING TIPS

If not properly socialized and trained, even a well-bred poodle will exhibit bad behaviors such as jumping up, barking, chasing, chewing and other destructive behaviors. You can prevent these habits

> **Did You Know?**
>
> **Once your poodle understands what behavior goes with a specific cue,** start weaning her off the food treats. At first, give a treat after each exercise. Then, start to give a treat only after every other exercise. Mix up times when you offer a food reward and when you only offer praise. This way your dog will never know when she is going to receive food and praise, or only praise.

and help your poodle become the perfect dog you've wished for by following some basic training and behavior guidelines.

Be consistent. Consistency is important, not just in terms of what you allow your poodle to do (get on the sofa, perhaps) and not do (jump up on people), but also in the verbal and body language cues you use with your dog and in his daily routine.

Be gentle but firm. Positive training methods are very popular. Properly applied, dog-friendly methods are wonderfully effective, creating canine-human relationships based on respect and cooperation.

Manage behavior. All living things repeat behaviors that are rewarded. Behaviors not reinforced will go away.

Provide adequate exercise. A tired poodle is a well-behaved poodle. Many behavior problems can be avoided, others resolved, by providing your poodle with enough exercise.

THE THREE-STEP PROGRAM

Perhaps it's too late to give your dog consistency, training and management from the start. Maybe he came from a poodle rescue shelter or you didn't realize the importance of these basic guidelines when he was a puppy. He already may have learned some bad behaviors. Perhaps they're even part of his genetic package. Many problems can be modified with ease using the following three-step process for changing an unwanted behavior.

Step No. 1: Visualize the behavior you want your dog to exhibit. If you simply stop your poodle from doing something, you leave a behavior vacuum. You need to fill that vacuum with something, so your dog doesn't return to the same behavior or fill it with one that's even worse! If you're tired of your dog jumping up, decide what

NOTABLE & QUOTABLE

If you want to make your dog happy, create a digging spot where she's allowed to disrupt the earth. Encourage her to dig there by burying bones and toys, and helping her dig them up. — Pat Miller, a certified dog trainer and owner of Peaceable Paws dog-training facility in Hagerstown, Md.

you'd prefer instead. A dog who greets people by sitting politely in front of them is a joy to own.

Step No. 2: Prevent your poodle from being rewarded for the behavior you don't want him to exhibit. Management to the rescue! When your poodle jumps up to greet you or get your attention, turn your back and step away to show him that jumping up no longer works in gaining your attention.

Step No. 3: Generously reinforce the desired behavior. Keep in mind that dogs will repeat behaviors that generate rewards. If your poodle no longer gets attention for jumping up and is heavily reinforced with attention and treats for sitting, he will offer sits instead of jumping, because he's learned that sitting will get him what he wants.

COUNTER CONDITIONING

The three-step process helps to correct those behaviors that temporarily gives your poodle satisfaction. For example, he jumps up to get attention; he countersurfs because he finds good food on counters; he nips at your hands to get you to play with him.

The steps don't work well when you're dealing with behaviors that are based in strong emotion, such as aggression and fear, or with hardwired behaviors such as chasing prey. With these, you can change the emotional or hardwired response through counter conditioning — programming a new emotional or automatic response to the stimulus by giving it a new association. Here's how you would counter condition a poodle who chases after skateboarders while you're walking him on a leash.

1. Have a large supply of high-value treats, such as canned chicken.

2. Station yourself with your poodle on a leash at a location where skateboarders will pass by at a subthreshold distance "X" — that is, where your poodle is alerted to the approaching person but doesn't bark.

3. Wait for a skateboarder. The instant your poodle notices the skateboarder, feed him bits of chicken, nonstop, until the skateboarder is gone. Stop feeding him.

4. Repeat many times until, when the skateboarder appears, your poodle looks at you with a big grin as if to say, "Yay! Where's my chicken?" This is a conditioned emotional response, or CER.

5. When you have a consistent CER at distance X, decrease the distance slightly, perhaps minus 1 foot, and repeat until you consistently get the CER at this distance.

6. Continue decreasing the distance and obtaining a CER at each level, until a skateboarder zooming right past your poodle elicits the "Where's my chicken?" response. Now go back to distance X and add a second skateboarder. Continue this process of desensitization until your poodle doesn't turn a hair at a bevy of skateboarders.

LEAVE IT ALONE

Most dogs enjoy eating, which makes it easy to train them using treats. But there's a downside to their gastronomic gusto — some dogs will gobble down anything even remotely edible. This could include fresh food, rotten food, things that once were food and any item that's ever been in contact with food. So, if you don't want your poodle gulping trash, teach him to leave things alone when told.

Place a tempting tidbit on the floor and cover it with your hand (gloved against teeth, if necessary). Say your cue word ("leave it" or "nah"). Your dog might lick, nibble and paw your hand; don't give in or you'll be rewarding bad manners.

Be careful in the timing of your treats. A common mistake is to reward at the wrong time. If you reach in your pocket for a food treat and your dog gets up, do not give a treat. Otherwise, he will interpret your reaching in your pocket for complying with the stay cue. — Judy Super, a professional dog trainer in Minneapolis, Minn.

SMART TIP!

It's a good idea to enroll your poodle in an obedience class if one is available in your area. Many areas have dog clubs that offer basic obedience training and preparatory classes for obedience competition. There are also local dog trainers who offer similar classes.

Wait until he moves away, then click or praise, and give a treat. Do not let your dog eat the food that's on the floor, only the treats you give him. Repeat until your poodle stops moving toward the tempting food.

Lift your hand momentarily, letting your dog see the temptation. Say the cue word. Be ready to protect the treat but instantly reward him if he resists temptation. Repeat, moving your hand farther away and waiting longer before clicking and rewarding.

Increase the difficulty gradually — practice in different locations, add new temptations, drop treats from standing height, drop several at a time and step away.

Remember to use your cue word, so your poodle will know what he's expected to do. Always reward good behavior! Rehearse this skill daily for a week. After that, you'll have enough real-life opportunities to practice.

Even the best dogs have some bad habits. If you are frustrated with a particular behavior that your poodle exhibits, don't despair! Go online and join Club Poodle, where you can ask other poodle owners for advice on dealing with excessive digging, stubbornness, house-training issues and more. Log on to **DogChannel.com/Club-Poodle** and click on "Community."

BAD BEHAVIOR

D iscipline — training one to act in accordance with rules — brings order to life. It is as simple as that. Without discipline, particularly in a group society, chaos reigns supreme and the group will eventually perish. Humans and canines are social animals and need some form of discipline in order to function effectively. Dogs need discipline in their lives in order to understand how their pack (you and other family members) functions and how they must act in order to survive.

Living with an untrained poodle is a lot like owning a piano that you do not know how to play; it is a nice object to look at but it does not do much more than that to bring you pleasure. Now, try taking piano lessons and suddenly the piano comes alive and brings forth magical sounds and rhythms that set your heart singing and your body swaying.

The same is true of your poodle. Every dog is a big responsibility, and if not sensibly trained may develop unacceptable behaviors that cause family problems.

Did You Know?

Anxiety can make a puppy miserable. Living in a world with scary monsters and suspected poodle-eaters roaming the streets has to be pretty nerve-wracking. The good news is that timid dogs are not doomed to be forever ruled by fear. Owners who understand a timid poodle's needs can help her build self-confidence and a more optimistic view of life.

The golden rule of dog training is simple. For each "question" (cue), there is only one correct "answer" (reaction). One cue equals one reaction. Keep practicing the cue until your dog reacts correctly without hesitation. Be repetitive but not monotonous. Dogs get bored just as people do; a bored dog's attention will not be focused on the lesson.

To train your poodle, you can enroll in an obedience class to teach him good manners as you learn how and why he behaves the way he does. You will also find out how to communicate with your poodle and how to recognize and understand his communications with you. Suddenly your dog takes on a new role in your life; he is interesting, smart, well behaved and fun to be with. He demonstrates his bond of devotion to you daily. In other words, your poodle does wonders for your ego because he constantly reminds you that you are not only his leader, you are his hero!

Those involved with teaching dog obedience and counseling owners about their dogs' behavior have discovered interesting facts about dog ownership. For example, training dogs when they are puppies results in the highest success rate in developing well-mannered and well-adjusted adult. Training an older poodle, from 6 months to 6 years, can produce almost equal results, providing that the owner accepts the dog's slower learning rate and is willing to patiently work to help him succeed. Unfortunately, many owners of untrained adult dogs lack the patience necessary, so they do not persist until their dogs are successful at learning particular behaviors.

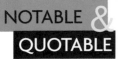
The best way to get through to dogs is through their stomach and mind — not the use of force. You have to play a mind game with them.

— Sara Gregware, a professional dog handler and trainer in Goshen, Conn.

Training a 10- to 16-week-old poodle pup (20 weeks maximum) is like working with a dry sponge in a pool of water. The pup soaks up whatever you teach him and constantly looks for more to do and learn. At this early age, his body is not yet producing hormones, and therein lies the reason for such a high success rate. Without hormones, he is focused on you and is not particularly interested in investigating other places, dogs, people, etc.

You are his leader; his provider of food, water, shelter and security. Your poodle latches onto you and wants to stay close. He will usually follow you from room to room, won't let you out of his sight when you are outdoors with him and will respond in like manner to the people and animals you encounter. If you greet a friend warmly, he will happily greet the person as well. If, however, you are hesitant, even anxious, about the approaching stranger, he will also respond accordingly.

Once your puppy begins to produce hormones, his natural curiosity emerges and he begins to investigate the world around him. It is at this time when you may notice your untrained dog begins to wander away and ignore your cues to stay close.

There are usually training classes within a reasonable distance of your home, but you also can do a lot to train your dog yourself.

Did You Know?

Dogs do not understand our language. They can be trained, however, to react to a certain sound, at a certain volume. Never use your poodle's name during a reprimand, as she might come to associate it with a bad thing!

Sometimes classes are available but the tuition is too costly, whatever the circumstances, information about training your poodle without formal obedience classes lies within the pages of this book. If the recommended procedures are followed faithfully, you can expect positive results that will prove rewarding for both you and your dog.

Whether your new poodle is a puppy or a mature adult, the teaching methods and training techniques used in basic behaviors are the same. No dog, whether puppy or adult, likes harsh or inhumane training methods. All creatures, however, respond favorably to gentle motivational methods and sincere praise and encouragement.

The following behavioral issues are those most commonly encountered. Remember, every dog and situation is unique. Because behavioral abnormalities are the leading reason for owners' abandoning their pets, we hope that you will make a valiant effort to solve your poodle's behavioral issues.

NIP NIPPING

As puppies start to teethe, they feel the need to sink their teeth into anything — unfortunately that includes your fingers, arms, hair, toes, whatever happens to be available. You may find this behavior cute for about the first five seconds — until you feel just how sharp those puppy teeth are.

Nipping is something you want to discourage immediately and consistently with a firm "No!" (or whatever number of firm "nos" it takes for your dog to understand that you mean business) and replace your finger with an appropriate chew toy.

STOP THAT WHINING

A puppy will often cry, whine, whimper, howl or make some type of commotion when he is left alone. This is basically his way of

Your poodle may howl, whine or otherwise vocalize her displeasure at your leaving the house and her being left alone. This is a normal case of separation anxiety, but there are things that can be done to eliminate this problem. Your dog needs to learn that she will be fine on her own for a while and that she will not wither away if she isn't attended to every minute of the day.

In fact, constant attention can lead to separation anxiety in the first place. If you are endlessly coddling and cuddling your poodle, she will come to expect this from you all of the time, and it will be more traumatic for her when you are not there.

To help minimize separation anxiety, make your entrances and exits as low-key as possible. Do not give your poodle a long, drawn-out goodbye, and do not lavish her with hugs and kisses when you return. This will only make her miss you more when you are away. Another thing you can try is to give your dog a treat when you leave; this will keep her occupied, her mind off the fact that you just left and help her associate your leaving with a pleasant experience.

You may have to acclimate your poodle to being left alone in intervals, much like when you introduced her to her crate. Of course, when your dog starts whimpering as you approach the door, your first instinct will be to run to her and comfort her, but don't do it! Eventually, she will adjust and be just fine — if you take it in small steps. Her anxiety stems from being placed in an unfamiliar situation; by familiarizing her with being alone, she will learn that she will be just fine.

When your poodle is alone in the house, confine her in her crate or a designated dog-proof area. This should be the area in which she sleeps, so she will already feel comfortable there and this should make her feel more at ease when she is alone. This is just one of the many examples in which a crate is an invaluable tool for you and your poodle, and another reinforcement of why your dog should view her crate as a happy place of her own.

Do not carry your puppy to her potty area. Lead her there on a leash or, better yet, encourage her to follow you to the spot. If you start carrying her, you might end up doing this routine for a long time, and your puppy will have the satisfaction of having trained you.

calling out for attention, of calling out to make sure that you know he is there and that you have not forgotten about him. He feels insecure when he is left alone; for example, when you are out of the house and he is in his crate, or when you are in another part of the house and he cannot see you.

The noise he is making is an expression of the anxiety he feels at being alone, so he needs to be taught that being alone is OK. You are not actually training your poodle to stop making noise, you are training him to feel comfortable when he is alone and thus removing the need to make the noise.

This is where his crate with a cozy blanket and a toy comes in handy. You want to know that your pup is safe when you are not there to supervise the best place for him to be is in his crate, rather than roaming about the house. In order for your pup to stay in his crate without making a fuss, he needs to be comfortable there. On that note, it is extremely important that the crate is never used as a form of punishment, or your poodle puppy will have a negative association with his crate.

Acclimate your puppy to his crate in short, gradually increasing time intervals. During these periods, put him in the crate, maybe with a treat, and stay in the room with him. If he cries or makes a fuss, do not go to him, but stay in his sight. Gradually, he will real-

ize staying in his crate is all right without your help and it will not be so traumatic for him when you are not around. You may want to leave the radio on softly when you leave the house; the sound of human voices can comfort him.

CHEW ON THIS

The national canine pastime is chewing! Every dog loves to sink his "canines" into a tasty bone, but anything will do! Dogs chew to massage their gums, make their new teeth feel better and exercise their jaws. This is a natural behavior deeply imbedded in all things canine. Owners should not stop their dog's chewing, but redirect it to chew-worthy objects. A smart owner will purchase proper chew toys for their poodle, like strong nylon bones made for large dogs. Be sure that these devices are safe and durable because your dog's safety is at risk.

The best solution is prevention: That is, put your shoes, handbags and other alluring objects in their proper places (out of the reach of the growing canine mouth). Direct puppies to their toys whenever you see them tasting the furniture legs or the leg of your pants. Make a loud noise to attract your poodle pup's attention and immediately escort him to his chew toy and engage him with the toy for at least four minutes, praising and encouraging him all the while.

NO MORE JUMPING

Jumping is a dog's friendly way of saying hello! Some owners don't mind when their dog jumps, which is fine for them. The problem arises when guests arrive and the dog greets them in the same manner — whether they like it or not! However friendly the greeting may be, chances are your visitors will not appreciate your dog's enthusiasm. Your dog will not be able to distinguish upon

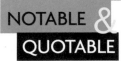

Stage false departures. Pick up your car keys and put on your coat, then put them away and go about your routine. Do this several times a day, ignoring your dog while you do it. Soon, her reaction to these triggers will decrease.

— September Morn, a dog trainer and behavior specialist in Bellingham, Wash.

whom he can jump and whom he cannot. Therefore, it is probably best to discourage this behavior entirely.

Pick a cue such as "off" (avoid using "down" because you will use that for your dog to lie down) and tell him "off" when he jumps. Place him on the ground on all fours and have him sit, praising him the whole time. Always lavish him with praise and petting when he is in the sit position, that way you are still giving him a warm, affectionate greeting, because you are as pleased to see him as he is to see you!

UNWANTED BARKING MUST GO

Barking is how dogs communicate. It can be somewhat frustrating because it is not easy to tell what your dog means by his bark: is he excited, happy, frightened, angry? Whatever it is your dog is trying to say, he should not be punished for barking. It is only when barking becomes excessive, and when excessive barking becomes a bad habit, that the behavior needs to be modified.

If an intruder came into your home in the middle of the night and your dog barked a warning, wouldn't you be pleased? You would probably deem your dog a hero, a wonderful guardian and protector of the home. On the other hand, if a friend unexpectedly drops by, rings the doorbell and is greeted with a sudden sharp bark, you would probably be annoyed at your dog. But isn't it the same behavior? Your dog doesn't know any better … unless he sees who is at the door and it is someone he is familiar with, he will bark as a means of vocalizing that his (and your) territory is being threatened. While your friend is not posing a threat, it is all the same to your dog. Barking is his means of letting you know there is an intruder, whether friend or foe, on your property. This type of barking is instinctive and should not be discouraged.

Excessive, habitual barking, however, is a problem that should be corrected early on. As your poodle grows up, you will be able to tell when his barking is purposeful and when it is for no reason, you will able to distinguish your dog's different barks and with what they are associated. For example, the bark when someone comes to the door will be different from the bark when he is excited to see you. It is similar to a person's tone of voice, except that your poodle has to completely rely on tone because he does not have the benefit of using words. An incessant barker will be evident at an early age.

There are some things that encourage barking. For example, if your dog barks nonstop for a few minutes and you give him a treat to quiet him, he believes you are rewarding him for barking. He will

now associate barking with getting a treat, and will keep barking until he receives his reward.

FOOD STEALING AND BEGGING

Is your poodle devising ways of stealing food from your cupboards? If so, you must answer the following questions: Is your dog really hungry? Why is there food on the coffee table? Face it, some dogs are more food-motivated than others; some are totally obsessed by a slab of brisket and can only think of their next meal. Food stealing is terrific fun and always yields a great reward — food, glorious food!

Therefore, the owner's goal is to make the reward less rewarding, even startling! Plant a shaker can (an empty can with a lid and filled with coins) on the table so that it catches your pooch off-guard. There are other devices available that will surprise your dog when he is looking for a mid-afternoon snack. Such remote-control devices, though not the first choice of some trainers, allow the correction to come from the object instead of you. These devices are also useful to keep your snacking poodle from napping on forbidden furniture.

Just like food stealing, begging is a favorite pastime of hungry pups with the same reward — food! Dogs learn quickly that humans love that feed-me pose and that their owners keep the good food for themselves. Why would humans dine on kibble when they can cook up sausages and kielbasa? Begging is a conditioned response related to a specific stimulus, time and place; the sounds of the kitchen, cans and bottles opening, crinkling bags and the smell of food preparation will excite your chowhound and soon his paws are in the air!

Here is how to stop this behavior: Never give in to a beggar, no matter how appeal-

Did You Know? Some natural remedies for separation anxiety are reputed to have calming effects, but check with your vet before use. Flower essence remedies are water-based extracts of different plants, which are stabilized and preserved with alcohol. A human dose is only a few drops, so seek advice from a natural healing practitioner on proper dosage for your poodle.

ing or desperate! By giving in, you are rewarding your dog for jumping up, whining and rubbing his nose into you. By ignoring your dog, you eventually will force the behavior into extinction. Note that his behavior will likely get worse before it disappears, so be sure there are not any "softies" in the family who will give in to your poodle every time he whimpers "Please."

DIG THIS

Digging, seen as a destructive behavior by humans, is actually quite a natural behavior in dogs. Their desire to dig can be irrepressible and most frustrating. When digging happens, it is an innate behavior redirected into something the dog can do in his everyday life. In the wild, a dog would be actively seeking food, making his own shelter, etc. He would be using his paws in a purposeful manner for his survival. Because you provide him with food and shelter, he has no need to use his paws for these purposes and so the energy he would be using may manifest itself in the form of holes all over your yard and flower beds.

Perhaps your dog is digging as a reaction to boredom — it is somewhat similar to someone eating a whole bag of chips in front of the TV — because they are there and there is nothing better to do! Basically, the answer is to provide your dog with adequate play and exercise so his mind and paws are occupied, and so he feels as if he is doing something useful.

Of course, digging is easiest to control if it is stopped as soon as possible, but it is often hard to catch your dog in the act. If your poodle is a compulsive digger and is not easily distracted by other activities, you can designate an area on your property where it is OK for him to dig. If you catch him digging in an off-limits area of the yard, immediately bring him to the approved area and praise him for digging there. Keep a close eye on him so you can catch him in the act; that is the only way to make him understand where digging is permitted and where it is not. If you take him to a hole he dug an hour ago and tell him "no," he will understand that you are not fond of holes, dirt or flowers. If you catch him while he is stifle-deep in your tulips, that is when he will get your message.

POOP ALERT!

Humans find feces eating, aka *coprophagia*, one of the most disgusting behaviors that their dog could engage in; yet to your dog, it is perfectly normal. Vets have found that diets with low digestibility, containing relatively low levels of fiber and high levels of starch, increase *coprophagia*. Therefore, high-fiber diets may decrease the likelihood of your poodle puppy eating feces. To discourage this behavior, feed nutritionally complete food in the proper amount. If changes in his diet do not seem to work, and no medical cause can be found, you will have to modify his behavior through environmental control before it becomes a habit.

There are some tricks you can try, such as adding an unpleasant-tasting substance to the feces to make them unpalatable or adding something to your dog's food which will make it unpleasant tasting after it passes through your dog. The best way to prevent your dog from eating his stool is to make it unavailable; clean up after he eliminates and remove any stool from the yard. If it is not there, he cannot eat it.

Never reprimand your dog for stool eating, as this rarely impresses your dog. Vets recommend distracting your poodle while he is in the act. Another option is to muzzle your dog when he goes in the yard to relieve himself; this usually is effective within 30 to 60 days. *Coprophagia* is mostly seen in pups 6 to 12 months, and usually disappears around the dog's first birthday.

AGGRESSION

Aggression, when not controlled, always becomes dangerous. An aggressive poodle, no matter the size, may lunge at, bite or even attack a person or another dog. Aggressive behavior is not to be tolerated. It is more than just inappropriate behavior; it is not safe. It is painful for a family to watch their dog become unpredictable in his behavior to the point where they are afraid of him. While not all aggressive behavior is dangerous, growling and baring teeth can be frightening. It is important to ascertain why your dog is acting in this manner. Aggression is a display of dominance, and your dog should not have the dominant role in his pack, which is, in this case, your family.

It is important not to challenge an aggressive dog, as this could provoke an attack. Observe your poodle's body language. Does he make direct eye contact and stare? Does he try to make himself as large as possible: ears pricked, chest out, neck arched? Height and size signify authority in a dog pack — being taller or "above" another dog literally means that he is "above" in the social status. These body signals tell you that your poodle thinks he is in charge, a problem that needs to be addressed. An aggressive dog is unpredictable: You never know when he is going to strike and what he is going to do. You cannot understand why a dog that is playful and loving one minute is growling and snapping the next.

The best solution is to consult a behavioral specialist, one who has experience with poodles, if possible. Together, perhaps you can pinpoint the cause of your dog's aggression and do something about it. An aggressive dog cannot be trusted and a dog who cannot be trusted is not safe to have as a family pet. If, very unusually, you find that your dog has become untrustworthy and you feel it necessary to seek a new home with a more suitable family and environment, explain fully to the new owners all your reasons for rehoming the dog to be fair to all concerned. In the very worst case, you will have to consider euthanasia.

AGGRESSION TOWARD DOGS

A dog's aggressive behavior toward another dog sometimes stems from insufficient exposure to other dogs at an early age. In poodles, early socialization with other dogs is essential.

It is the breeder and owner's responsibility to curb and redirect any signs of aggression so that your poodle can become an upright member of canine society. If other dogs make your poodle nervous and agitated, he might use aggression as a defensive mechanism. A dog who has not received sufficient exposure to other canines tends to believe he is the only dog on the planet. He becomes so dominant that he does not even show signs that he is fearful or threatened. Without growling or any other physical signal as a warning, he will lunge at and bite another dog. A way to correct

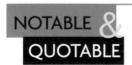

The purpose of puppy classes is for puppies to learn how to learn. The pups get the training along the way, but the training is almost secondary.

— *professional trainer Peggy Shunick Duezabou of Helena, Mont.*

this is to let your poodle approach another dog only when walking on a leash. Watch very closely and at the very first sign of aggression, correct your dog and pull him away. Scold him for any sign of discomfort, and praise him when he ignores or tolerates the other dog. Keep this up until he stops the aggressive behavior, learns to ignore other dogs or accepts other dogs. Praise him lavishly for his correct behavior.

DOMINANT AGGRESSION

A social hierarchy is firmly established in a wild dog pack; dogs want to dominate those under him and please those above him. They know there must be a leader. If you are not the obvious choice for emperor, your dog will assume the throne! These conflicting, innate desires are what you are up against when training your dog. In training a dog to obey cues, you are reinforcing the fact that you are the top dog in the "pack" and that your dog should, and should want to, serve his superior. Thus, you are suppressing your dog's urge to dominate by modifying his behavior and making him obedient.

An important part of training is taking every opportunity to reinforce that you are the leader. The simple action of making your poodle sit to wait for his food says you control when he eats and that he is dependent on you for food. Although it may be difficult, do not give in to your dog's wishes every time he whines at you or looks at you with his pleading eyes. It is a constant effort to show your dog that his place in the pack is at the bottom. This is not meant to sound cruel or inhumane. You love your poodle and you should treat him with care and affection. You certainly did not get a dog just so you could boss around another creature. Dog training is not about being cruel or feel-

ing important, it is about molding your dog's behavior into what is acceptable and teaching him to live by your rules. In theory, it is quite simple: catch him in appropriate behavior and reward him for it. Add a dog into the equation and it becomes a bit more trying, but as a rule of thumb, positive reinforcement works best.

With a dominant dog, punishment and negative reinforcement can have the opposite effect of what you are trying to achieve. It can make your dog fearful and/or act out aggressively if he feels he is being challenged. Remember, a dominant dog perceives himself at the top of the social heap and will fight to defend his perceived status. The best way to prevent that is to never give him reason to think he is in control in the first place. If you are having trouble training your poodle and it seems as if he is constantly challenging your authority, seek the help of an obedience trainer or behavioral specialist. A professional will work with both you and your dog to teach you effective techniques to use at home. Beware of trainers who rely on excessively harsh methods; scolding is necessary now and then, but the focus in your training should always be positive reinforcement.

If you can isolate what brings out your poodle's fear reaction, you can help him get over it. Supervise your poodle's interactions with people and other dogs, and praise him when it goes well. If he starts to act aggressively in a situation, correct him and remove him from the situation. Do not let people approach your dog and start petting him without your expressed permission. That way, you can have your dog sit to accept petting and praise him when he behaves appropriately; you are focusing on praise and modifying his behavior by rewarding him. By being gentle and by supervising his

interactions, you are showing him that there is no need to be afraid or defensive.

SEXUAL BEHAVIOR

Dogs exhibit certain sexual behaviors that may have influenced your choice of male or female when you first purchased your poodle. To a certain extent, spaying/neutering will eliminate these behaviors, but if you are purchasing a dog that you wish to breed, you should be aware of what you will have to deal with throughout your dog's life.

Female dogs usually have two estruses per year with each season lasting about three weeks. These are the only times in which a female dog will mate, and she usually will not allow this until the second week of the cycle, but this does vary from female to female. If not bred during the heat cycle, it is not uncommon for a female to experience a false pregnancy, in which her mammary glands swell and she exhibits maternal tendencies toward toys or other objects.

Smart poodle owners must also recognize that mounting is not merely a sexual expression. It is also one of dominance. Be consistent and persistent in your training, and you will find that you can "move mounters."

One of the best ways to nurture a cooperative and solid relationship with your poodle is to become involved in an enjoyable activity. A bored poodle can easily become a troublesome dog.

Deciding what recreation activity you and your poodle would enjoy the most takes some consideration. Do you want a sport, such as agility, where you and your dog are both active participants? Would you prefer an activity, such as flyball, where your dog does most of the running? Does something less physical, such as visiting senior citizens, sound more like your cup of tea? Perhaps a brief synopsis of some of the more popular dog-friendly recreations will help you narrow down the choices.

EXERCISE OPTIONS

All poodles need exercise to keep them physically and mentally healthy. An inactive dog is an overweight dog, who will likely suffer joint strain or torn ligaments. Inactive dogs also are prone to mischief and may do anything to relieve their boredom. This often leads to behavioral problems, such as chewing or barking. Regular daily exercise, such as walks and play sessions, will keep your poodle slim, trim and happy.

Provide your poodle with interactive play that stimulates his mind as well as his body.

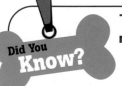

Did You Know?

The Fédération Internationale Cynologique is the world kennel club that governs dog shows in Europe and elsewhere around the world.

SMART TIP!

Before You Begin
Because of the physical demands of sporting activities, a poodle puppy shouldn't begin official training until she is done growing. That doesn't mean, though, that you can't begin socializing her to sports. Talk to your veterinarian about what age is appropriate to begin.

It's a good idea to have a daily period of one-on-one play, especially with a puppy or young dog. Continue this type of interaction throughout your dog's life, and you will build a lasting bond. Even senior poodles need the stimulation that activity provides.

If your poodle is older or overweight, consult your veterinarian about how much and what type of exercise he needs. Usually, a 10- to 15-minute walk once a day is a good start. As the pounds start to drop off, your dog's energy level will rise, and you can increase the amount of daily exercise.

Whether a dog is trained in the structured environment of a class or alone with his owner at home, there also are many sporting activities that can bring fun and rewards to owner and dog once they have mastered basic training techniques.

AGILITY TRIALS

Agility is a fast-growing sport, attracting dogs of all kinds and their equally diverse owners. In agility, the dog, off leash but guided by the handler, runs a course of obstacles including jumps, tunnels, A-frames, elevated boards (called dog walks) and more. Basically, the dog must negotiate the obstacles in proper order and style and do it within a set time. As in obedience, the team can strive for high honors, titles only or simply the joy of working together.

Agility has plenty of fun obstacles — from jumps to tunnels to turns to hoops — that are sure to keep your poodle enthused.

Most training facilities require that dogs have some basic obedience before entering an agility class because your dog must be responsive to you and reliable about not interfering with other dogs and handlers or running off. It is also important to allow your puppy to mature before undertaking agility's jumps and sharp turns because young bones and joints are injured more easily than mature ones.

Again, multiple organizations sponsor agility titles at all levels, from novice through advanced. The rules, procedures and obstacles vary somewhat among the organizations, so, again, it's important to obtain and read the appropriate rule book before entering your dog in competition. In addition to the American Kennel Club and United Kennel Club, the United States Dog Agility Association and the North American Dog Agility Council also offer agility trials and titles. Toy and Miniature Poodles can participate in Teacup Dogs Agility Association, which uses scaled-down obstacles for the tiny competitors.

The AKC offers Novice Agility, Open Agility, Agility Excellent and Master Agility Excellent titles. To achieve an MX title, a dog must first earn the AX title, then earn qualifying scores in the agility excellent class at 10 licensed or member agility trials.

The USDAA offers eight agility titles. An Agility Dog has achieved three clear rounds (no faults) under two different judges in the starters or novice category of competition. An Advanced Agility Dog has achieved three clear rounds under two different judges in the Advanced class. The Masters Agility Dog has demonstrated versatility by achieving three clear rounds under two different judges in the masters standard agility class.

In addition, a dog must receive a qualifying score at the masters level in each of the following: Gamblers Competition, to demonstrate proficiency in distance control and handling; Pairs or Team Relay, to demonstrate cooperative team effort and good sportsmanship; Jumping Class, to demonstrate jumping ability and fluid working habit; and Snooker Competition, to further demonstrate a dog and handler's versatility in strategic planning. To earn a Jumpers Master, Gamblers Master, Snooker Master or Relay Master title, a dog must achieve five clear rounds in the appropriate class. A USDAA Agility Dog Champion (ADCh.) has earned the MAD, SM, GM, JM and RM titles. The USDAA also recognizes the Agility Top 10 annually.

USDAA promotes competition by hosting major tournament events each year, including its Grand Prix of Dog Agility championships. The Dog Agility Masters Team Pentathlon Championship promotes agility as a team sport, and the Dog Agility Steeplechase championship focuses on speed in performance. Dogs must be registered with the USDAA in order to compete in its events.

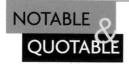

Poodles have a sense of humor — a delight of life that should never be trained out of them. You have to know when to insist they work and when to give a little; it's a fine line.
— Standard Poodle owner Kim Duda, director of training at Columbus (Ohio) All-Breed Training Club

The USDAA also offers programs for older dogs and younger handlers. The Veterans Program is for dogs 7 years of age or older. The Junior Handler Program is for handlers up to 18 years of age and is designed to encourage young people to participate in dog agility as a fun, recreational family sport.

The North American Dog Agility Council offers certificates of achievement for the regular, jumpers and gamblers classes. The purpose of the regular agility class is to demonstrate the handler and dog's ability to perform all of the agility obstacles safely and at a moderate rate of speed. At the open level, the goal is to test the handler and dog's ability to perform the obstacles more quickly and with more directional and distance control and obstacle discrimination.

At the elite level, more complex handler strategies are tested, with the dog moving at a brisk pace. The dog may be entered in the standard, veterans or junior handlers division. In all divisions, certification in the regular agility classes will require three qualifying rounds under at least two different judges. NADAC also awards the Agility Trial Champion title.

OBEDIENCE TRIALS

Obedience trials in the United States trace back to the early 1930s, when organized obedience training was developed to demonstrate how well dogs and their owners could work together. Helen Whitehouse Walker, a Standard Poodle fancier, pioneered obedience trials after she modeled a series of exercises after the Associated Sheep, Police and Army Dog Society of Great Britain. Since Walker initiated the first trials, competitive obedience has grown by leaps and bounds, and today more than 2,000 trials are held in the United States every year, with more than 100,000 dogs competing. Any registered AKC or UKC dog can enter an obedience trial for the club in which he is registered, regardless of conformational disqualifications or neutering.

Obedience trials are divided into three levels of progressive difficulty. At the first level, Novice, the dogs compete for the title of Companion Dog; at the intermediate level, Open, dogs compete for a Companion Dog Excellent title; and at the Advanced level, dogs compete for a Utility Dog title. Classes are subdivided into "A" (for beginners) and "B" (for more experienced handlers). A perfect score at any level is 200, and a dog must score 170 or better to earn a "leg," three of which are needed to earn the title. To earn points, the dog must score more than 50 percent of the available points in each exercise; the possible points range from 20 to 40.

Once a dog has earned the Utility Dog title, he can compete with other proven obedience dogs for the coveted title of Utility Dog Excellent, which requires that the dog win "legs" in 10 shows. In 1977, the title Obedience Trial Champion was established by the AKC. Utility Dogs who earn legs in Open B and Utility B earn points toward their Obedience Trial Champion title. To become an OTCh., a dog needs to earn 100 points, which requires three first place wins in Open B and Utility B under three different judges.

The grand prix of obedience trials, the AKC National Obedience Invitational, gives qualifying Utility Dogs the chance to win the newest and highest title: National Obedience Champion. Only the top 25 ranked obedience dogs, plus any dog ranked in the top three in his breed, are allowed to compete.

RALLY BEHIND RALLY

Rally is a sport that combines competition obedience with elements of agility, but is less demanding than either one of these activities. Rally was designed keeping the average dog owner in mind and is easier than many other sporting activities.

At a rally event, dogs and handlers are asked to move through 10 to 20 different stations, depending on the level of competition. The stations are marked by numbered signs, which tell the handler the exercise to be performed. The exercises vary from making different types of turns to changing pace.

Dogs can earn rally titles as they get better at the sport and move through the different levels. The titles to strive for are Rally Novice, Rally Advanced, Rally Excellent and Rally Advanced Excellent.

To get your poodle puppy prepared to enter a rally competition, focus on teaching him basic obedience, for starters. Your dog must know the five basic obedience cues — sit, down, stay, come and heel — and perform them well. Next, you can enroll your dog in a rally class. Although he must be at least 6 months of age to compete in rally, you can start basic training long before his 6-month birthday.

TRACKING TALES

Tracking, by nature, is a vigorous, noncompetitive outdoor sport. The AKC awards titles for registered dogs trained to track, but even if you don't want to

SMART TIP!

If you find your poodle isn't suited for group activities, once you get your veterinarian's OK and basic obedience training behind you, you and your poodle can find plenty of opportunities for exercise, training and strengthening the bond between you right in your own backyard.

pursue a title, training your poodle to track can be great fun, providing exercise for you and your dog and giving you the opportunity to observe the incredible powers of the canine nose. Poodles have good, busy noses — as you know if you've ever taken one for a walk. You may as well put that talent to use! The best way to train is with other people and their dogs; if you can find a tracking club, all the better. Some obedience clubs also have groups of people interested in training their dogs to track.

The purpose of a tracking test is to demonstrate the dog's ability to recognize and follow human scent. Before a dog is permitted to enter a tracking test, his handler must obtain a written statement certifying that the dog has satisfactorily performed a certification test within one year of the date the test is to be held. The statement must be signed by a person approved by the AKC to judge tracking tests. The certification test should be of a complexity equivalent to the tracking test and take place under conditions similar to such a test.

A Tracking Dog title is given to a dog who has been certified by two judges to have passed a licensed or member club tracking test. To earn a TD, the dog must track a per-

son 440 to 500 yards away with three to five changes of direction. The track is laid 30 minutes to two hours before the dog begins scenting. A Tracking Dog Excellent title requires two passes of the Tracking Dog Excellent tracking test. The TDX track is three to five hours old when the dog begins and is 800 to 1,000 yards long with five to seven changes of direction as well as cross-tracks by other people. The Variable Surface Tracking title is designed to test a dog's real-world tracking skills in urban and wilderness settings. To earn the VST, a dog must follow a three- to five-hour-old track that may take it down streets, through buildings and empty lots or other realistic terrains where there may be lots of competing scents. Finally, the AKC will issue a CT title to a dog who has earned all three tracking titles.

Competitive sport or just plain fun, make sure your poodle gets plenty of exercise.

SHOW DOGS

When you purchase your poodle puppy, you must make it clear to the breeder whether you want one just as a lovable companion and pet, or if you hope to purchase a poodle with show prospects. No reputable breeder will sell you a puppy and tell you that he will definitely be show quality because so much can change during the early months of a puppy's development. If you do plan to show, what you hopefully will have acquired is a puppy with show potential.

To the novice, exhibiting a poodle in the ring may look easy, but it takes a lot of hard work and devotion to win at a show such as the annual Westminster Kennel Club Dog Show in New York City, not to mention a fair amount of luck, too!

The first concept that the canine novice learns when watching a dog show is that each dog first competes against members of his own breed. Once the judge has selected the best dog in each breed (Best of Breed), the chosen dog will compete with other dogs in his group (such as Terrier, Non-Sporting, Working, etc.). Finally, the dogs chosen first in each group will compete for the Best In Show title.

The second concept you must understand is that the dogs are not actually compared against one another. The judge compares each dog against the breed standard, the written description of the ideal dog approved by the AKC. While some early breed standards were indeed based on specific dogs who were famous or popular, many dedicated enthusiasts say that a perfect specimen as described in the standard has never walked into a show ring, has never been bred and, to the woe of dog breeders around the globe, does not exist. Breeders attempt to get as close to this ideal as possible with every litter, but theoretically the "perfect" dog is so elusive that it is impossible. (Even if the perfect dog were born, breeders and judges probably would never agree that he was perfect!)

If you are interested in exploring the world of conformation, your best bet is to join your local breed club or the national

Teaching your poodle to watch your every move begins when you first bring her home. Puppies will follow you, even without a leash, because they want to be with you, especially if you have a treat in your hand. Keep your dog on your left side and offer her a small piece of food with each step you take. In no time, your pup will think that you're an automatic treat dispenser, and she will never leave your side.

(or parent) club, the Poodle Club of America. These clubs often host regional and national specialties, shows only for poodles, which can include conformation as well as obedience and field trials. Even if you have no intention of competing with your poodle, a specialty is like a festival for lovers of the breed who congregate to share their favorite topic: poodles! Clubs also send out newsletters, and some organize training days and seminars providing owners the opportunity to learn more about their chosen breed. To locate the breed club closest to you, contact the AKC, which furnishes the rules and regulations for all of these events, plus general dog registration and other basic requirements of dog ownership.

CANINE GOOD CITIZEN

If obedience work sounds too regimented but you'd still like your poodle to have a title, prepare him for the Canine Good Citizen test. This program is sponsored by the AKC, with tests administered by local dog clubs, private trainers and 4-H clubs.

To earn a CGC title, your poodle must be well-groomed and demonstrate the manners that all good dogs should exhibit. The CGC test requires a dog to follow the sit, lie down, stay and come cues, react appropriately to other dogs and distractions, allow a stranger to approach him, sit politely for petting, walk nicely on a loose leash, move through a crowd without going wild, calm down after play or praise and sit still for an examination by the judge. Rules are posted on the AKC's website.

THERAPY

Visiting nursing homes, hospices and hospitals with your dog can be a tremendously satisfying experience. Many times,

Poodle Pleasures

Thanks to the poodle's multi-tasking skills, there is an entire world of canine sports and activities that awaits you.

Dock jumping: A thrilling sport for the water-loving Standard Poodle, a dockdog performs a long jump by leaping off a dock of specified proportions to retrieve a toy thrown by her handler. The length (or height) of the jump is measured from the edge of the dock. The Dockdog organization also offers titling.

Flyball: Furiously fast, this relay race consists of a box loaded with tennis balls that ejects a ball whenever a dog jumps against the release. Four hurdles, set at a height appropriate for the shortest canine on the team of four, precede the box. Each dog individually leaps across the hurdles, hits the release, catches the ball and repeats her path back to the handler. The North American Flyball Association awards titles and maintains statistics.

Backpacking: Backpacking provides an excellent conditioning activity that burns off Standard Poodle energy while you enjoy a healthy hike. Dogs need properly fitted equipment to prevent discomfort and chafing as they carry water, snacks or their own food for overnight trips. Several organizations offer backpacking titles, including the Dog Scouts of America.

Freestyle: Frequently referred to as "dancing with your dog," the harmonious teamwork between owner and dog seen in this sport would dazzle Fred Astaire. Freestyle deftly blends music, dance and dog training into an enjoyable, crowd-pleasing presentation. Individual teams combine traditional obedience moves with leg kicks, swirls, bows and a variety of imaginative moves. The Canine Freestyle Federation and the World Canine Freestyle Organization award titles.

Carting, Sledding, Skijoring, Scootering: Different approaches to pulling sports than weight pull, each of the aforementioned activities utilize a Standard Poodle's strength and are coupled with firm obedience. Carting offers the most likelihood for titling; the rest mainly provide your poodle with great exercise and fun.

Sports are physically demanding. Have your vet perform a full examination of your poodle to rule out joint problems, heart disease, eye ailments and other maladies. Once you get the green light, start having fun in your new dog-sporting life!

a dog can reach an individual who has otherwise withdrawn from the world. The poodle can be a delightful therapy dog.

Although a gentle disposition is definitely a plus, the often normally rambunctious dog seems to instinctively become gentler when introduced to those who are weak or ailing. Some basic obedience is, of course, a necessity for the therapy dog and a repertoire of tricks is a definite bonus. The sight of a clownish poodle "hamming it up" can help brighten most anyone's day.

Most facilities require a dog to have certification from a therapy dog organization. Therapy Dog International and the Delta Society are two such organizations. Generally speaking, if your dog can pass a Canine Good Citizen test, earning certification will not be difficult. Certified therapy dog workers frequently get together a group and regularly make visitations in their area.

Poodles in all three varieties dominate conformation events.

My dogs and I love tracking in the outdoors and walking through the woods as they follow a scent, earning turkey hot dogs for hunting and finding dropped articles. What could be better? — Toy Poodle owner Debbie Smith of Belpre, Ohio

Smart owners can find out more information about this popular and fascinating breed by contacting the following organizations. They will be glad to help you dig deeper into the world of poodles, and you won't even have to beg!

American Kennel Club: The AKC website offers information and links to conformation, tracking, rally, obedience and agility programs, member clubs and all things dog. www.akc.org

Canadian Kennel Club: Our northern neighbor's oldest kennel club is similar to the AKC in the states. www.ckc.ca

Canine Performance Events: Sports for dogs to keep them active. www.k9cpe.com

Dog Scouts of America: Take your dog to camp. www.dogscouts.com

Love on a Leash: Your poodle has a lot of love to give. www.loveonaleash.org

National Association of Professional Pet Sitters: Hire someone to watch your dog when you leave town. www.petssitters.org

North American Dog Agility Council: This site provides links to clubs, obedience trainers and agility trainers in the United States and Canada. www.nadac.com

The Poodle Club of America: All three sizes are represented in this club. www.poodleclubofamerica.org

Teacup Dogs Agility Association: Toy and Miniature Poodles can participate in this scaled-down version of agility. www.k9tdaa.com

Therapy Dogs Inc.: Get your poodle involved in therapy. www.therapydogs.com

Therapy Dogs International: Find more therapy dog info here: www.tdi-dog.org

United Kennel Club: The UKC offers several of the events offered by the AKC, including agility, conformation and obedience. In addition, the UKC offers competitions in hunting and dog sport (companion and protective events). Both the UKC and the AKC offer programs for junior handlers, ages 2 to 18. www.ukcdogs.com

United States Dog Agility Association: The USDAA has lots of information about training, clubs and events in the United States, Canada, Mexico and overseas. www.usdaa.com

World Canine Freestyle Organization: Dancing with your dog is fun! www.worldcaninefreestyle.org

BOARDING

So you want to take a family vacation — and you want to include all members of the family. You usually make arrangements for accommodations ahead of time anyway, but this is imperative when traveling with a dog. You do not want to make an overnight stop at the only place around for miles only to discover that the hotel doesn't allow dogs. Also, you don't want to reserve a room for your family without confirming

it's a **Fact** The **American Kennel Club** was established in 1884. It is America's oldest kennel club. The **United Kennel Club** is the second oldest in the United States and began registering dogs in 1898.

Some communities have created regular dog runs and separate spaces for small dogs. These small-dog runs are ideal for introducing puppies to the dog park experience. The runs are smaller, the participants are smaller and their owners are often more vigilant because they are used to watching out for their fragile companions.

that you are traveling with a poodle because if it is against the hotel's policy, you may not have a place to stay.

Alternatively, if you are traveling and choose not to bring your poodle, you will have to make arrangements for him. Some options are to leave him with a family member or a neighbor, have a trusted friend stop by often or stay at your house. Another option is leaving your poodle at a reputable boarding kennel.

If you choose to board your poodle at a kennel, visit in advance to see the facilities and check how clean they are, and where the dogs are kept. Talk to some of the employees and see how they treat the dogs. Do they spend time with the dogs either during play or exercise? Also, find out the kennel's policy on vaccinations and what they require. This is for all of the dogs' safety because when dogs are kept together, there is a greater risk of diseases being passed between them.

To maximize your fun, vacations should, if possible, include your pet.

Remember to keep your dog's leash slack when interacting with other dogs. It is not unusual for a dog to pick out one or two canine neighbors to dislike. If you know there's bad blood, step off to the side and find a barrier, such as a parked car, between the dogs. If there are no barriers to be had, move to the side of the walkway, cue your poodle to sit, stay and watch you until her nemesis passes; then continue your walk.

HOME STAFFING

For the poodle parent who works all day, a pet sitter or dog walker may be the perfect solution for the lonely pet pooch longing for a midday stroll. Dog owners can approach local high schools or community centers if they don't have a neighbor who is interested in a part-time commitment.

When you interview potential dog walkers, consider their experience with dogs, as well as your poodle's rapport with the candidate. (Poodles can be excellent judges of character.) You should always thoroughly check all references before entrusting your poodle — and opening your home — to a new dog walker.

For an owner's long-term absence, such as a business trip or vacation, many poodle owners welcome the services of a pet sitter. It's usually less stressful on the dog to stay home with a pet sitter than to be boarded in a kennel. Pet sitters also may be more affordable than a week's stay at a full-service doggie day care.

Pet sitters must be even more reliable than dog walkers because the dog is depending on his surrogate owner for all of his needs over an extended period. Owners are advised to hire a certified pet sitter through the National Association of Professional Pet Sitters. NAPPS provides online and toll-free pet sitter locator services. The nonprofit organization only certifies serious-minded, professional individuals who are knowledgeable in canine behavior, nutrition, health and safety. Whether or not you take your poodle with you, always keep your poodle's best interest at heart when planning a trip.

SCHOOL'S IN SESSION

Puppy kindergarten, which is usually open to dogs between 3 to 6 months of age, allows puppies to learn and socialize with other dogs and people in a structured setting. Classes helps to socialize your poodle so that he will enjoy going places with you and be a well-behaved member in public gatherings. They prepare him for adult obedience classes and for a lifetime of social experiences he will have with your friends and his furry friends. The problem with most puppy kindergarten classes is that they only occur one night a week.

If you're home during the day, you may be able to find places to take your puppy so he can socialize. Just be careful about dog parks and other places that are open to any dog. An experience with a dog bully can undo all the good your training classes have done.

If you work, your puppy may be home alone all day, a tough situation for a poodle. Chances are he can't hold himself that long, so your potty training will be undermined — unless you're teaching him to use an indoor potty. Also, by the time you come home, he'll be bursting with energy, and you may think that he's hyperactive and uncontrollable.

Don't think your poodle is too cool for school! Get him involved in a dog sport or obedience classes.

The only suitable answer for the working professional with a poodle is doggie day care. Most large cities have some sort of day care, whether it's a boarding kennel that keeps your dog in a run or a full-service day care that offers training, play time and even spa facilities. They range from a person who keeps a few dogs at his or her home to a state-of-the-art facility built just for dogs. Many of the more sophisticated doggie day cares offer webcams so you can see what your dog is up to throughout the day. Things to look for:

- escape-proof facilities, such as gates in doorways that lead outside
- inoculation requirements for new dogs
- midday meals for young dogs
- obedience training, using reward-based methods
- safe and comfortable nap areas
- screening of dogs for aggression
- small groups of similar sizes and ages
- toys and playground equipment, such as tunnels and chutes
- trained staff, with an adequate number to supervise the dogs (no more than 10 to 15 dogs per person)
- a webcam

CAR TRAVEL

You should accustom your poodle to riding in a car at an early age. You may or may not

Before you turn on the ignition, make sure everyone is buckled up, including your poodle!

take him in the car often, but at the very least he will need to go to the vet once in a while, and you do not want these trips to be traumatic for your dog or troublesome for you. The safest way for a poodle to ride in the car is in his crate. If your dog uses a crate in the house, you can use the same crate for travel.

Another option is a specially made safety harness for dogs, which straps your poodle in the car much like a seat belt would. Do not let the dog roam loose in the vehicle; this is very dangerous! If you should make an abrupt stop, your dog can be thrown and injured. If your dog starts climbing on you while you are driving, you will not be able to concentrate on the road. It is an unsafe situation for everyone — human and canine.

For long trips, stop often to let your poodle relieve himself. Take along whatever you need to clean up after him, including some paper towel should he have an accident in the car or suffer from motion sickness.

IDENTIFICATION

Your poodle is your valued companion and friend. That is why you always keep a close eye on him, and you have made sure that he cannot escape from the yard or wriggle out of his collar and run away from you. However, accidents can happen and there may come a time when your poodle unexpectedly gets separated from you. If this should occur, the first thing on your mind will be finding him. Proper identification, including an ID tag, a tattoo and possibly a microchip, will increase the chances of his being returned to you safely and quickly.

An ID tag on a collar or harness is the primary means of identifying a lost pet (and ID licenses are required in many cities). Although inexpensive and easy to read, collars and ID tags can come off or be taken off.

A microchip doesn't get lost. The microchip is embedded underneath the dog's skin and contains a unique ID number that is read by scanners. It comes in handy for identifying lost or stolen pets. However, to be effective, the microchip must be registered in a national database. Smart owners will register their dog and regularly check that their contact information is kept up-to-date.

However, one thing to keep in mind is that not every shelter or veterinary clinic has a scanner, nor do most folks who might pick up and try to return a lost pet.

Your best best? Get both!

POODLE, a Smart Owner's Guide™

part of the Kennel Club Books® Interactive Series™

JOIN OUR
ONLINE
**Club
Poodle**™

LIBRARY OF CONGRESS CATALOGING-IN-PUBLICATION DATA

Poodle / from the editors of Dog fancy magazine.
    p. cm. — (Smart owner's guide)
Includes bibliographical references and index.
ISBN 978-1-59378-773-8
1. Poodles. I. Dog fancy (San Juan Capistrano, Calif.)
SF429.P85P65 2010
636.72'8—dc22

        2009046639